YOU'RE USED TO RUNNING YOUR OWN SHOW—NOW TAKE CHARGE OF YOUR FINANCIAL FUTURE. THIS PROFESSIONAL GUIDE TO FINANCIAL SUCCESS PROVIDES:

- Self-diagnostic reviews to help you evaluate your overall financial profile
- Tools to organize your personal records
- Debt management and spending control
- Tips on insurance coverage and tax breaks for self-employed professionals and small business owners
- The best investment portfolio for you
- Retirement objectives and plans
- Work sheets and action plans
- Ten simple things to do to help you achieve financial peace of mind in the 1990s
  . . . AND MORE

COMPLETE, COMPREHENSIVE, AND PERSONALIZED

**POND'S
PERSONALIZED FINANCIAL PLANNING
GUIDE FOR
SELF-EMPLOYED PROFESSIONALS AND SMALL
BUSINESS OWNERS**

Look for these other Pond's Personalized Financial Planning Guides
by Jonathan D. Pond

■

POND'S PERSONALIZED FINANCIAL PLANNING GUIDE FOR
SALESPEOPLE

■

POND'S PERSONALIZED FINANCIAL PLANNING GUIDE FOR
DOCTORS, DENTISTS, AND HEALTH-CARE PROFESSIONALS

■

POND'S PERSONALIZED FINANCIAL PLANNING GUIDE FOR
TEACHERS AND EMPLOYEES OF EDUCATIONAL INSTITUTIONS

POND'S PERSONALIZED FINANCIAL PLANNING GUIDE FOR SELF-EMPLOYED PROFESSIONALS AND SMALL BUSINESS OWNERS

JONATHAN D. POND

A DELL TRADE PAPERBACK

To Laura

A DELL TRADE PAPERBACK

Published by
Dell Publishing
a division of
Bantam Doubleday Dell Publishing Group, Inc.
666 Fifth Avenue
New York, New York 10103

ISBN: 0-440-50397-3

Design: Stanley S. Drate/Folio Graphics Co., Inc.

Printed in the United States of America

Published simultaneously in Canada

September 1991

10   9   8   7   6   5   4   3   2   1

RRH

ACKNOWLEDGMENTS

Numerous people have participated in the preparation of this book, although they may not realize how helpful they have been. Over the past decade I have spoken and worked with many self-employed professionals and small business owners. While each may have thought that his or her individual financial circumstances were unique, there turns out to be a great deal of commonality of financial needs among the self-employed. This book focuses on those shared needs and concerns.

Viveca Gardiner was instrumental in assisting with the research and preparation of this book, and her many contributions are gratefully acknowledged.

I also sincerely appreciate the wonderful and insightful guidance of my two editors at Dell, Jody Rein and Jeanne Cavelos.

My family was very understanding of my long absences. Perhaps special recognition should be given to my new daughter, Laura, who arrived on the scene in the midst of my writing. Without her "help" this book would have been published several months earlier.

CONTENTS

INTRODUCTION

People spend more time thinking about personal money matters than about any other single subject, according to a recent survey. I know from my work that people do worry a lot about their personal finances, but even I thought money matters would rank second as far as what adults like to think about. Personal financial planning is an important subject for everyone. After all, we work hard for our money, we want to retire comfortably. Yet turning that money into financial security is no easy task, one made even harder by the supposed complexity of personal finance and by our being bombarded, day in and day out, with often conflicting, often biased financial advice. While counseling members of various occupations on financial planning matters, I began to see that working in a particular occupation presents a variety of unique financial planning opportunities and problems. For example, I have found that self-employed professionals and small business owners are often so busy with their businesses that they don't spend enough time tending to important personal financial planning matters. Since most of these people cannot realistically expect their business interest to provide them with financial security for the rest of their lives, they *need* to pay more attention to their personal finances. This book, directed solely to the money concerns of self-employed professionals and small business owners, will help you make good use of your limited time in addressing your own personal circumstances so that it will be easier for you to take action to achieve financial security.

This book will help self-employed professionals* and owners

---

*Self-employed professionals are persons who are licensed by their state to practice their professions and who practice independently. Self-employed professionals include, but are not limited to, architects, barbers, electricians, engineers, funeral directors, plumbers, and public accountants.

of small businesses do a better job with their money. While
independent businesspeople aren't much different from members of other occupations—insofar as everyone wants to achieve
financial security—they do share some unique characteristics
that can and should influence the course of their personal financial planning. For example:

- Independent businesspeople are often so busy with their work
  that they lack the time and, often, the knowledge needed to
  manage their personal finances effectively.
- Small business owners often have a substantial portion if not
  most of their wealth tied up in the business. Difficult though it
  may seem, these owners should take action to accumulate
  resources outside of the business in order to provide for long-
  term financial security.
- Because they are self-employed, independent businesspeople
  must assure that they obtain comprehensive and continuous
  personal insurance coverage, whether through their business
  or through other sources.
- Self-employed people can avail themselves of a number of tax-
  saving opportunities not generally available to employees.
- Retirement planning is particularly crucial for self-employed
  professionals and small business owners. Many fail to plan
  adequately for retirement even though particularly advan-
  tageous retirement plans are often available to them.

You may not have paid a lot of attention to financial planning
up to now, or you may think your finances are under control.
Either way, this book contains a variety of work sheets and self-
diagnostic reviews that will help you see where you stand. Even
if you find you are in relatively good financial shape, the numerous suggestions in these pages will help you do a better job.

While money is the focal point, successful personal financial
planning encompasses a variety of areas, including:

- Setting financial objectives and planning to meet them
- Organizing your personal records
- Managing your debt effectively and bringing your spending
  under control
- Saving and investing regularly
- Accumulating an investment portfolio that meets your needs
- Minimizing income taxes
- Planning to achieve a comfortable retirement
- Preparing and keeping up-to-date appropriate estate planning
  documents

All these topics, and more, are covered in this book. The advantage of a book written just for independent businesspeople is your not having to wade through a lot of material that doesn't pertain to your unique circumstances. This is not a get-rich-quick book, however; it is a get-rich-*sensibly* book. Hopefully, you will find a lot of common sense on these pages, because common sense is the key to successful personal financial planning. Even if you rely on financial advisers to handle much of your planning, this book will still be of benefit because, no matter how much you rely on others to assist you, you need to take control of your financial future.

Don't be surprised if you find the financial planning process to be rather daunting. There is a lot to be done, even if your finances are in pretty good shape. The work sheets and action plans will help you identify areas that need attention. You won't be able to do everything, and matters that need attention cannot be addressed all at once. But begin to do one or a few things and you will find you *can* improve your personal financial status. And it isn't such a burden after all. In fact, it should be fun to watch your investments grow, to know that your debt and spending are under control, to know that you are adequately insured, and to realize that you will be able to enjoy a long and financially fruitful retirement.

Achieving success in your personal finances is not unlike achieving success in your business endeavors. They both require *focus* and *follow-through*. Just as you focus on the most important and pressing matters in your business, you need to focus on key areas of financial planning. But, as you know from your business activities, focus is not enough. Neither is it enough in your personal financial planning. Just as you follow through with problems and opportunities in your business, you also need to follow through in your financial planning by monitoring your progress toward achieving financial security. While you may need to rely on professional assistance from time to time, only you know how you want to structure your financial life. Your basic goals and desires are the center of your personal financial life, and this book will help you translate these goals into financial terms and achieve them, bringing you a lifetime of financial peace of mind.

I

GETTING
ORGANIZED

1

Isn't It Time to Take Stock of Your Personal Financial Well-Being?

—

Why do small business owners and self-employed professionals need their own money book? You probably don't need to learn about fancy investment techniques and elaborate tax-avoidance strategies (although you may have tried them without much success), so I won't address them. If you are like many independent businesspeople, you have not paid sufficient attention to your *personal* finances, instead spending most of your waking hours worrying about business matters. You can learn to focus on important personal money matters with a minimum investment of your time. You probably need to devote more time to your own financial situation, to ensure that you achieve financial security. This book is *not* about business finances. Instead, it guides you through the process of achieving financial peace of mind by recognizing that self-employed people and business owners usually have some unique personal financial problems—and opportunities.

This book is written especially for you. It won't burden you with matters that pertain to people in other occupations or whose general financial circumstances are very different from yours. In fact, each chapter highlights areas unique to independent businesspeople and, more important, tells you how to take advantage of the financial opportunities and deal with the financial problems that are relevant to self-employed people.

THE FRAMEWORK OF PERSONAL FINANCIAL PLANNING

Successful personal financial planning requires attention to three distinct yet interrelated areas: getting organized, accumulating wealth, and planning for later life. Within each area are several important matters you should be concerned about. These are discussed in the chapters that follow.

I.   Getting organized
   - Setting financial objectives, planning to meet them, and revising them when your circumstances change
   - Determining where you stand financially
   - Putting your personal records in order
   - Taking control of your financial future
   - Finding competent financial advisers
   - Acquiring and maintaining comprehensive and cost-effective insurance coverage
   - Planning to meet major expenses
   - Managing your debt effectively
   - Bringing your spending under control

II. Accumulating wealth
   - Saving and investing regularly, independent of resources invested in your business
   - Setting realistic investment objectives
   - Learning to take advantage of the numerous investment alternatives available
   - Accumulating an investment portfolio that meets your needs
   - Managing your investment portfolio
   - Minimizing current income taxes
   - Planning to reduce future income taxes

III. Planning for later life
   - Starting to plan early for a comfortable retirement
   - Projecting retirement income and expenses
   - Taking advantage of tax-advantaged retirement plans
   - Coordinating your retirement income needs with your personal and pension plan investments
   - Making sure your estate planning documents are valid and up-to-date
   - Assuring an orderly disposition of your business in the event of your death
   - Determining if more elaborate estate planning techniques will benefit you and your heirs
   - Dealing with the problems of old age—both yours and your parents'

You might think this very long list of items would require you to work full-time just on your personal finances, and you don't have very much spare time as it is. But, as you will see in this and succeeding chapters, personal financial planning really isn't that complicated (although a lot of financial institutions and financial planners would like you to believe otherwise). All it takes is some discipline, a little time, and the willingness either to be your own financial planner or to make sure your financial planning adviser(s) are acting in your best interests. If successful financial planning can be boiled down to two words, they are *common sense*. If you think back on the dumb things you have done with your money in the past—and all of us have done dumb things with our money on occasion—you will find that the debacles were caused by lapses of common sense. I hope you find a lot of common sense in these pages. If you're looking for no-risk ways to get rich quickly, read no further. If you're looking for ways to get rich sensibly or to achieve lifetime financial security by the time you retire, you'll benefit from the advice that follows.

DECIDING WHAT YOU WANT TO ACCOMPLISH

Two things in life that you had better not think of in financial terms: children and pets. *Example:* If I had a $10,000 car, I wouldn't spend ten times that amount, or $100,000, on repairs. But I just spent $250 for an eye operation on my $25 dog.

SETTING GOALS

One thing you should do if you haven't already is establish some financial planning goals. What do you want to accomplish in your financial life? Permit me to tell you what your primary financial planning goal is: financial security. Financial security means you can live the rest of your life without having to work. Most people don't achieve financial security until they retire, and there is nothing wrong with this. What is unfortunate, however, is the number of people who never achieve financial security— not by age 65, not by age 75, never. And don't think that just because you operate your own business you are somehow pre- destined to achieve financial security. As you are undoubtedly aware, many businesses, particularly service businesses, do not create a great deal of value in and of themselves. You hope they will allow you the luxury of an income large enough to accumulate sufficient resources for financial security. Whatever your situation, achieving financial security requires a lot of planning and some sacrifice: unless your business can be built up to the point where it can be sold for a princely sum, the only way you're going to reach the universal goal of financial security is to accumulate investments independent of the business. This requires saving, and the only way to save regularly is to spend less than you earn, which, in essence, means you have to *live beneath your means*. Many independent businesspeople have trouble living beneath their means. They work very hard and therefore feel entitled to live the good life. Sometimes this is a recipe for financial disappointment in later life.

Beyond the long-term goal of financial security, you probably have a variety of other financial planning objectives. Among the more common are:

- Saving more regularly
- Improving personal record keeping
- Making sure savings are invested wisely
- Reducing personal debt
- Assuring complete insurance coverage
- Buying a home
- Purchasing or starting another business
- Making a major purchase
- Reducing income taxes
- Meeting the children's college education costs
- Retiring early
- Providing support for elderly parents
- Transferring assets to children
- Making sure the estate is properly planned

You should be pretty specific about the goals you have and how you plan to go about achieving them. Be sure to write them down from time to time. To encourage you to do this, the following work sheet provides space to list your personal financial goals. Your most important goal has already been entered.

DEVELOPING STRATEGIES TO ACHIEVE YOUR GOALS

Strategies are detailed plans that help you *achieve* your financial goals. It's easy to set goals, but it's much harder to devise strategies to achieve them. For example, many business owners want to retire early, but far fewer are able to come up with a plan

FINANCIAL GOALS WORK SHEET

Date: _____

1. Achieve financial security by age _____.

2. _____

3. _____

4. _____

5. _____

6. _____

7. _____

that will allow them to do this—and comfortably. Even people who devise a realistic strategy often end up not sticking with it.

SETTING PRIORITIES

Establishing priorities is essential because some goals are probably more urgent than others. Achieving financial security by retirement age is your first priority, but what's next? Many people would rank securing adequate insurance coverage pretty far down the list of priorities, yet it is so essential to financial security, it should be a very high priority. Insufficient insurance may jeopardize years of past—or future—savings, and many independent businesspeople are not adequately insured.

COPING WITH "LIFE EVENTS"

Over the course of your lifetime, you will experience several "life events" that will probably make it necessary to reevaluate your personal financial status and plans. They will usually require you to make some adjustment in your planning; some—divorce, for example—may require major changes. Table 1 lists life events that most commonly lead to at least some modification of your plans.

Note that many of these circumstances are quite common. In fact, you could lead a very typical life and experience eight to ten such events.

The nature and extent of changes required by life events

TABLE 1

Life Events That Usually Require a Modification in Financial Plans

---

FAMILY
Marriage
Birth or adoption of children
Family member with special financial needs
Aging parents
Death of a spouse or other close family member
Receipt of an inheritance
Cohabitation
Separation/divorce

OCCUPATIONAL
Beginning a career
Purchasing or starting a business
Changing careers
Downturn in business
Business subject to fluctuating income
Unemployment

HEALTH
Disability
Old age
Chronic illness
Terminal illness

---

vary. For some you will need the counsel of competent professionals, but they usually cannot be expected to address all necessary changes. While it is difficult to generalize about such a multiplicity of events, the following financial planning areas are often affected by the changed circumstances:

Budgeting and record keeping. Review/revise personal budgets, prepare projections, including income tax ramifications, based on changed status

Insurance. Review beneficiary designations, adequacy of coverage, and type of coverage

Credit. Establish or reestablish credit standing, revise loan documentation

Family assets. Review holdings, change ownership designations, evaluate sufficiency of diversification

Estate planning. Review/revise estate planning documents and estate planning techniques, clarify/change bequests to heirs

MINIMIZING MARITAL MONEY SQUABBLES

When was the last time you argued with your spouse or significant other about money? If you want to have an argument, money matters are an omnipresent and very convenient catalyst. But money disputes do not necessarily indicate deeper problems. Actually, the vast majority of couples agree on important, longer-term family financial matters. The disagreements tend to be over smaller day-to-day financial matters. There are a couple of easy things you can do to minimize interspousal money tensions.

First, you should set aside one day each year to sit down with your spouse, review your financial status, and make some plans for the next year. The date you select shouldn't be around tax-return preparation time, however. That's already stressful enough on couples. Efficient and comprehensive record keeping throughout the year will make this "day of reckoning" much easier.

Second, you should work with your spouse to develop the financial goals discussed earlier in this chapter. Most financial matters don't just take care of themselves. To accomplish your goals, you will have to know what they are and work toward them together.

What all this boils down to, of course, is improved communication with your spouse. Lack of communication about family finances, or, for that matter, in any aspect of marriage, is a recipe for strife. But don't expect the arguments to go away entirely. Chances are you and your spouse will always have somewhat different approaches toward family money management. In fact, if you think about it, spenders tend to marry savers. While these couples may never eliminate marital money strife completely, they can, with a little communication, turn these bellicose extremes into a happier medium.

BEING HAPPY WITH WHAT YOU'VE GOT

There is far too much preoccupation with money these days. Most people waste a lot of time thinking they would be on Easy

> Show me a married couple who has never had an argument about money, and I'll show you a couple on the way to their wedding reception.

Street if only they earned $10,000 more than they do currently. What a difference a generation makes. Our parents were certainly more content. What's so wrong with our being happy with what we've got?

We all want financial security, of course. Believe it or not, some people spend all they earn during their working years thinking they'll be able to live off Social Security when they're retired. But Social Security will support most people only about one week of each month. Assuming you'd like to provide for the other three weeks as well, you must either build up your business to a level where it can fetch a lot of money when it is sold or, more likely, accumulate a sizable investment portfolio by the time you retire. If you are like most independent businesspeople and need to accumulate investments outside your business, you have to save regularly. In order to save regularly, you have to spend less than you earn.

No matter how obvious that sounds, many of us have difficulty doing it, but the best way to spend less than you earn is to be happy with what you've got. A lot of people don't like to hear this. They want a fancier car or an imported kitchen or an exotic vacation or a larger house. After all, the advertisers tell us we have to have these things to be happy, and, by golly, our neighbors have some of these things, and they sure seem happy. That's baloney, of course. The neighbors, even the ones who do make $10,000 more per year than you do, probably feel the same way about you as you feel about them. In fact, they probably envy you for being your own boss. If you can be happy with what you've got, you'll find it a lot easier to save the money to make the investments that will allow you to achieve financial security. It's as simple as that.

SETTING YOUR RECORDS STRAIGHT

Since you are a business owner, you already know how important it is to maintain good business records. Why, then, are the personal records of so many businesspeople in such disarray? Many rationalize by saying "I spend so much time straightening out my business records, I don't have the energy to straighten them out at home." These people don't know how simple an effective home record-keeping system can be. A good system is one that is comprehensive enough to be effective, yet simple enough to encourage regular use. You should think of organizing your records around three basic files: a safe-deposit box, a home active file, and a home inactive file. Don't make the mistake of commingling your business records with your personal records. They'll be almost impossible to untangle at tax time. The following Personal Record-Keeping Organizer work sheet will guide you in the process of organizing your home records.

PERSONAL RECORD-KEEPING ORGANIZER

The following Personal Record-Keeping Organizer serves two purposes. First, you can indicate next to each item where that particular item is now located. Second, you can organize your personal records by consolidating your documents into the three "files" noted below.

I. ITEMS FOR STORAGE IN SAFE-DEPOSIT BOX

PERSONAL
1. Family birth certificates
2. Family death certificates
3. Marriage certificate
4. Citizenship papers
5. Adoption papers
6. Veteran's papers
7. Social Security verification

OWNERSHIP
1. Bonds and certificates
2. Deeds
3. Automobile titles
4. Household inventories
5. Home-ownership records
   (e.g., blueprints, deeds, surveys,
   capital addition records, yearly records)
6. Copies of trust documents

OBLIGATION/CONTRACT
1. Contracts
2. Copies of insurance policies
3. IOUs
4. Retirement and pension-plan documents

COPIES OF ESTATE PLANNING DOCUMENTS
1. Wills _____
2. Living wills _____
3. Trusts _____
4. Letters of instruction _____
5. Guardianship arrangements _____

II. ITEMS FOR STORAGE IN HOME ACTIVE FILE

CURRENT INCOME/EXPENSE DOCUMENTS
1. Unpaid bills _____
2. Current bank statements _____
3. Current broker's statements _____
4. Current canceled checks and money-order
   receipts _____
5. Credit card information _____

CONTRACTUAL DOCUMENTS
1. Loan statements and payment books _____
2. Appliance manuals and warranties
   (including date and place of purchase) _____
3. Insurance policies:
   - Home _____
   - Life _____
   - Automobile _____
   - Personal liability _____
   - Health and medical _____
   - Other: _____ _____
4. Receipts for expensive items not yet paid for _____

PERSONAL
1. Employment records _____
2. Health and benefits information _____
3. Family health records _____
4. Copies of wills _____
5. Copies of letters of instruction _____
6. Education information _____
7. Cemetery records _____
8. Important telephone numbers _____
9. Inventory and spare key to safe-deposit box _____

10. Receipts for items under warranty _____
11. Receipts for expensive items _____

TAX
 1. Tax receipts _____
 2. Paid bill receipts
    (with deductible receipts filed separately to
    facilitate tax preparation and possibly reduce
    taxes) _____
 3. Brokerage transaction advices _____
 4. Income tax working papers _____
 5. Credit statements _____
 6. Income and expense records for rental
    properties _____
 7. Medical, dental, and drug expenses _____
 8. Records of business expenses _____

BUSINESS
 1. Business tax returns _____
 2. Business financial statements _____
 3. Keogh plan _____
 4. Simplified employee pension plan _____
 5. Buy-sell agreements _____
 6. Articles of incorporation _____
 7. Partnership agreements _____
 8. Company patents/copyrights _____
 9. Equipment-leasing agreement(s) _____
10. Insurance policies _____

III. ITEMS FOR STORAGE IN HOME INACTIVE FILE

1. Prior tax returns _____
2. Home improvement records _____
3. Brokerage advices (prior to three most recent
   years) _____
4. Family health records (prior to three most recent
   years) _____
5. Proof that major debts or other major contracts
   have been met _____
6. Canceled checks (prior to three most recent years) _____

Your *safe-deposit box* should include most of your legal and important personal papers, ownership records, and estate planning documents. Keep an updated list of the contents of the safe-deposit box in your active file. Incidentally, do you store valuables in your safe-deposit box? Did you know that the bank probably doesn't insure them? You need to obtain a safe-deposit-box insurance floater through the company that handles your homeowner's or renter's insurance.

Use an *active file* to monitor your current budget, organize bills, keep track of important papers, and help you in preparing the current year's tax return. Important business documents should also be stored in a separate section of your active file. Remember: If your filing system is not easy to use, you will end up postponing filing items, sometimes indefinitely. A good home active file could consist of nothing more than a cardboard box with manila file folders. You'll save time as well as money, since the chances of overlooking valuable tax deductions are smaller if your records are in order. Good personal records will also help you avoid problems if you are ever audited by the IRS.

The major reason for keeping an *inactive file* is to prove past tax returns. This file should contain important papers—formerly stored in your active file—that are more than three years old. After six years most people can safely discard their records, although you will want to keep receipts to back up any improvements you have made to your home. You may also want to keep old tax returns as a matter of curiosity—to show your great-grandchildren that it was once possible to live on less than $100,000 per year. At the present rate of inflation, they'll probably be earning $100,000 per *month*!

TAKING A SELF-AUDIT WITH PERSONAL FINANCIAL STATEMENTS

Since you operate your own business, you are also well aware of the importance of preparing business financial statements periodically. It is equally important to prepare personal financial statements. Two types of statements should suffice. First is a statement of personal assets and liabilities (balance sheet), which summarizes your assets, liabilities, and net worth. Second is a personal budget, which summarizes where your personal (not business) income comes from and how you spend (or, perhaps, fritter) it. You don't need an accountant to prepare your personal financial statements, although you do need to pull some records together. If your financial situation is quite complicated, however, you may ask your accountant to help you prepare them if you haven't already. A blank Statement of Personal Assets and Liabilities form is included to help you, and a Personal Budget Planner appears in Chapter 3.

STATEMENT OF PERSONAL ASSETS AND LIABILITIES

A statement of personal assets and liabilities is an excellent way to gauge your progress toward financial security. Be sure to list assets at their current market values, but be realistic when valuing real estate and personal possessions like cars and furniture. Be particularly careful in valuing your business. Many have an inflated opinion of the value of their businesses (just as homeowners often think their homes are worth a lot more than they really are). The danger in overvaluing your business is that you may be misled into thinking that proceeds from the sale of the business will provide a large portion of your retirement income needs. If you are going to have to rely on the sale of your business to assure your financial security, you should consider having the business professionally appraised from time to time.

If you own a lot of real estate and stock that have appreciated considerably in value, or if your business has appreciated considerably, remember that your net worth might not be as high as it seems if you eventually liquidate those assets since you will have to pay a capital gains tax on them. Finally, be sure to list all liabilities. People have a tendency to understate liabilities.

Once you have prepared an up-to-date balance sheet, you can then make plans to increase your net worth. If you are disappointed by the level (or absence) of your net worth, don't be dismayed. The important thing is to take action to improve it. That's why the Statement of Personal Assets and Liabilities has three columns. You should prepare it every six months or so, so that you can monitor the improvement in your net worth.

PERSONAL BUDGET

Budgeting your personal income and expenses is as important for your well-being as business budgeting is important for

---

If you maintained your business files the way you maintain your files at home, you'd be unemployable.

the well-being of your business. The purposes of personal budgeting are: (1) to define possible problems in the way you spend your money; (2) to identify opportunities to overcome these problems; and (3) to help you plan realistically to improve your spending habits. Knowing both the amount of income that can reasonably be expected and how that income is spent can go far in preventing the duress and domestic squabbles that often result from unforeseen financial burdens. Tips on controlling your spending and preparing a budget appear in Chapter 3.

TAKING CONTROL OF YOUR FINANCIAL FUTURE

You may have thought (until reading this book) that you weren't knowledgeable enough to manage your finances effectively. Or you may have thought that the demands of your own business were such that you didn't have time to plan. There are clear dangers in these perceptions. Lack of knowledge is no

---

STATEMENT OF PERSONAL ASSETS AND LIABILITIES

This form can be used to summarize your assets and liabilities. Three columns are included so that you can periodically monitor your progress. This statement should be prepared at least once per year (many people prepare it more frequently).

	19____	19____	19____
ASSETS			
1. Cash in checking and brokerage accounts	$..............	$..............	$..............
2. Money market funds and accounts	....	....	....
3. Fixed-income investments			
▪ Savings accounts	....	....	....
▪ Certificates of deposit (CDs)	....	....	....
▪ Government securities and funds	....	....	....
▪ Mortgage-backed securities and funds	....	....	....
▪ Corporate bonds and bond funds	....	....	....

	19	19	19
■ Municipal bonds and bond funds	....	....	....
■ Other fixed-income investments	....	....	....
4. Stock investments			
■ Common stock in publicly traded companies	....	....	....
■ Stock mutual funds	....	....	....
■ Other stock investments	....	....	....
5. Real estate investments			
■ Undeveloped land	....	....	....
■ Directly owned, income-producing real estate	....	....	....
■ Real estate limited partnerships	....	....	....
6. Ownership interest in your private business	....	....	....
7. Cash value of life insurance policies	....	....	....
8. Retirement-oriented assets			
■ Individual retirement accounts (IRAs)	....	....	....
■ Salary reduction 401(k) plans	....	....	....
■ Keogh or simplified employee pension plans	....	....	....
■ Vested interest in corporate pension and profit-sharing plans	....	....	....
■ Employee thrift and stock-purchase plans	....	....	....
■ Tax-deferred annuities	....	....	....
■ Other retirement-oriented assets	....	....	....
9. Personal assets			
■ Personal residence(s)	....	....	....
■ Automobile(s)	....	....	....
■ Jewelry	....	....	....
■ Personal property	....	....	....

	19	19	19
10. Other assets			
■	....	....	....
■	....	....	....
■	....	....	....
■	....	....	....
11. Total assets	$...............	$...............	$.............

LIABILITIES

	19	19	19
1. Credit cards and charge accounts	$...............	$...............	$. ....
2. Income taxes payable	....	....	....
3. Miscellaneous accounts payable	....	....	....
4. Bank loans	....	....	....
5. Policy loans on life insurance policies	....	....	....
6. Automobile loans	....	....	....
7. Student loans	....	....	....
8. Mortgages on personal residence	....	....	....
9. Mortgages on investment real estate	....	....	....
10. Broker's margin loans	....	....	....
11. Limited partnership debt	....	....	....
12. Other liabilities			
■	....	....	....
■	....	....	....
■	....	....	....
13. Total liabilities	$...............	$...............	$.............
14. Net worth (total assets less total liabilities)	$...............	$...............	$.............

Note: Assets should be listed at their current market values. Be realistic in valuing those assets that require an estimate of market value, such as your home and personal property.

---

excuse. As you will see, personal financial planning isn't that complicated. Lack of time is no excuse. Successful personal financial planning doesn't have to take a lot of time.

You probably need to take more control over your financial future. In order to do so, you need to:

- Learn more about and devote some time to your own finances.
- Select your legal, insurance, and investment advisers carefully.
- Avoid making mistakes with your money.

RUNNING YOUR OWN SHOW

Since you have your own business, you already know a lot more about personal finance than you may think, because managing your personal finances is not unlike managing a business. Just as with businesses, you need to control your spending, insure against the unforeseen, borrow judiciously, invest resources wisely and with a long-term perspective, minimize income taxes, and prepare for long-term financial viability. Each of these matters is too important to ignore or to abdicate to someone else to handle. Sources of information on managing your personal finances—in addition to this book—are available in daily newspapers, magazines, radio and television, and so on. Believe it or not, a lot of the information you receive from these sources is pretty good, as long as you don't feel compelled to act on every recommendation.

You may think you don't have the time to attend to all of your money matters. As you will see from this book, good personal financial planning doesn't require a lot of time. Most of the important areas—insurance, retirement forecasting, and estate planning—usually need only be addressed once or twice a year. You could be well rewarded for paying closer attention to the most dynamic area, investments; but, on the other hand, if you spend too much time studying the markets and reviewing your investments, you probably will be prone to the wrong decisions: when it comes to deciding what to do with a particular investment, often the best thing to do is nothing.

SELECTING AND MANAGING YOUR ADVISERS

Busy self-employed people all too often either fail to select appropriate financial advisers or neglect to manage them effectively. You probably need to take a more active role in making sure your advisers are providing the best possible advice and service. The three most common family advisers are discussed below.

Stockbroker. It is certainly no secret that stockbrokers have an inherent conflict of interest in advising you on your investments. You are usually better off buying and holding, whereas the broker not only has to generate transactions but also has additional incentive to promote products that his or her firm wants promoted. Nevertheless, there are many excellent stock-brokers who can deal with these conflicts and still act in your best interest. Often these are brokers who have established themselves in the business (versus a new broker, who is usually under an inordinate amount of pressure to generate commissions).

Once you have found a good broker, you need to state your investment parameters clearly. Firmly reject any suggested new investments or changes in your portfolio if you feel they are inappropriate. Do not get into the habit of simply consenting to all broker recommendations. Eventually, a good broker will understand your investment approach and a mutually satisfactory relationship will be formed.

Insurance agent. It is usually better to select an independent insurance agent who has the capability and willingness to shop among several carriers for the best possible coverage rather than one who represents a single company. The agent who handles your business insurance needs may or may not be well suited to handling your personal insurance needs. Insurance agents may have a conflict of interest in that certain insurance products pay much higher commissions than other, more mundane products. In the worst instances, mediocre agents may not even suggest essential coverage to you (umbrella liability insurance, for example) because it provides such a low commission. The better agents will review your coverage with you at least annually and will be willing to shop for appropriate policies. Moreover, effective agents will go to bat for you when necessary. For example, if you are having difficulty securing disability insurance because of a health problem, a good agent will work hard to find the necessary insurance at the best possible price. To assure a good relationship, you must keep the agent informed of changes in your circumstances, and, if necessary, insist on a periodic review of your coverage.

Attorney. You may not yet have a family attorney. But you'll need one at least to prepare necessary estate planning documents, such as wills and powers of attorney. You should probably use an attorney who is approximately your age or younger, since you will probably use the same attorney over the years and won't want to be burdened with finding a new lawyer when your current one retires. On the other hand, you may outgrow your attorney's expertise if your estate grows to a level that will benefit from more sophisticated estate planning techniques. These techniques usually require the expertise of an attorney who devotes all of his or her time to estate planning matters. The attorney you select should be responsive to your needs and should conduct his or her work in a timely manner.

Finding the right advisers is well worth the effort. There is no ideal way to locate these professionals, but word-of-mouth recommendation can be an important first step. Finally, if you're unhappy with one of your advisers, it may be because you have not taken an active role in the relationship. But if the problem persists, do not hesitate to make a change. It's amazing how many people dislike or distrust their advisers yet continue to do business with them.

DO YOU NEED A FINANCIAL PLANNER?

Financial planning is on everyone's mind these days and several hundred thousand people now hold themselves out as "financial planners." Some work on commissions, some work strictly on fees, and some collect both commissions and fees. You should expect to pay anywhere from $2,000 to $10,000 for a comprehensive and truly objective financial plan and consultations from a fee-based financial planner. While financial planning sounds like a service everyone could use, many people will not benefit significantly from the services of a financial planner. One reason is that most financial planners are simply not capable of dealing with the multiplicity of matters that affect your financial well-being, including insurance, investments, credit management, pensions, and estate planning.

Some self-employed professionals and small business owners, typically those with high incomes and/or high net worth, can certainly benefit from the process, but I firmly believe that many people can and should do their own financial planning. It requires a modest amount of reading and research combined with periodic reviews of family finances, much as described in this book. Incidentally, the whole process can be fun. Those who feel that they need a financial planner (perhaps for a particular problem rather than a comprehensive review) obviously have many to choose from. If you need to be assured of objectivity,

---

At the present rate of growth in the financial planning profession, by the year 2000 every man, woman, and child over the age of 3 in the United States will be a "financial planner."

consider selecting a certified public accountant (CPA) or estate planning attorney who are committed to the financial planning process. Some of them specialize in financial planning for self-employed people. As with all of your advisers, word-of-mouth recommendation is a good way to find competent financial planners.

AVOIDING MISTAKES IN YOUR PERSONAL FINANCES

Unfortunately, the road to financial security contains many potholes that can slow your progress, sometimes significantly. Just as the investment homily advises that the "best way to win in the stock market is by not losing," in financial planning the best way to achieve financial security is by avoiding mistakes. Remember, no one is perfect. We all do stupid things with our money from time to time. Listed below are ten common errors that many independent businesspeople make in the course of their financial life.

1. *Devoting too little attention to personal financial planning matters*. Self-employed professionals and small business owners often pay much too little attention to their own finances. Sure, you may be preoccupied with your business and may have precious little time to devote to anything else. Nevertheless, ignoring certain essential financial planning matters can be detrimental to both short-term and long-term financial security.

2. *Neglecting to cover gaps in insurance coverage*. The surest way to wipe out years of hard-earned accumulation of capital is to suffer an uninsured loss. Because, in essence, independent businesspeople pay for all their own insurance coverage, they often obtain insufficient coverage in certain key areas, such as long-term disability coverage and life insurance. Deficiencies in any area of insurance can be disastrous.

3. *Mismanaging credit*. Credit is very easy to obtain today, yet many people lack the self-discipline necessary to manage it effectively. Financial institutions are no help, by the way, as they promote high-limit credit cards, six-year car loans, and large home equity loans with repayment terms that are too liberal. Independent businesspeople are particuarly prone to credit problems because they often have to sign personally for business loans, and confronted with a business downturn, they all too readily borrow against personal assets to support the business.

4. *Failing to save regularly outside the business*. Unless you are confident that you can get rich from the sale of your business, regular saving outside the business is essential in achieving

financial security. As income increases, savings should increase. Nevertheless, many independent businesspeople do not save regularly. They shouldn't be surprised, therefore, when they find they can't afford to retire.

5. *Making dumb investments.* Whether because of ignorance or greed, or both, everyone makes an inappropriate investment at least once in his or her lifetime. The entrepreneurial inclinations of self-employed people often lead them to take too much risk in their outside investing, when, because of the risk inherent in business ownership, the opposite would be preferable. In other words, the self-employed person may need to make personal investments somewhat more conservatively than might otherwise be the case.

6. *Failing to take full advantage of the many tax breaks available to the self-employed.* Uncle Sam offers numerous tax breaks to self-employed people, but, unfortunately, many fail to take advantage of them. Good tax planning, which shouldn't be deferred until December of each year, is one of the easiest ways to save money.

7. *Failing to accumulate sufficient retirement resources.* Although small business owners and self-employed professionals can often avail themselves of tax-advantaged retirement plans, many neglect to do so. If they also neglect to accumulate sufficient resources outside these retirement plans, they may not have enough on hand to assure a comfortable retirement. Independent businesspeople must recognize that they are responsible for their own retirements and the sooner they begin preparing, the better.

8. *Neglecting to prepare wills and other estate planning documents.* While they may not be around to witness the havoc, people who do not prepare basic estate planning documents do their heirs a "grave" disservice. Good estate planning is particularly important for business owners because they need to plan for the orderly disposition of their business in the event of death. Inappropriate or nonexistent estate planning can end up costing heirs a great deal in terms of both inconvenience and money.

9. *Not shopping for the most appropriate financial planning products and services.* The explosion in the number and types of investment, insurance, and other financial products is bewildering, but with some effort people can find the right ones to meet their needs. However, many self-employed people are unwilling to take the time and/or gain a sufficient understanding to assure they are making the most of each dollar they spend or invest.

10. *Giving up control to financial advisers.* Many independent businesspeople make the mistake of abdicating responsibility for handling *their* money and financial affairs, deferring to various advisers. Although it is often appropriate to rely on the expertise of competent advisers, by not taking an active role in personal financial matters you will simply not receive the level of service you need and deserve.

No one can avoid making mistakes in personal financial planning. Some, however, make too many mistakes and, worse, repeat them. As you review the above list, identify areas where you need improvement and pay close attention when they are addressed later in this book. The Financial Planning and Record-Keeping Action Plan will help you keep track of steps you've dealt with successfully and steps that still require your attention. This Action Plan, as well as those at the end of each chapter, should be reviewed periodically to remain useful. At the end of each Action Plan there is space for you to make comments and list important items you need to focus on.

Now that you've established your objectives, organized your records, and determined where you stand financially, you're ready to start taking charge of your personal financial life. The first matter to discuss is insurance, because without appropriate personal insurance coverage, everything else in your financial life, including you and your business, is in jeopardy.

The key to achieving riches beyond your wildest imagination: Never own anything that eats.

FINANCIAL PLANNING AND RECORD-KEEPING ACTION PLAN

CURRENT STATUS

Needs Action   *Okay or Not Applicable*

☐ ☐ 1. Take the time necessary to evaluate your *personal* financial status periodically, independent of the financial status of your business.

☐ ☐ 2. Set some realistic financial planning goals, and plan how you are going to achieve them.

☐ ☐ 3. If you experience any major changes in your personal or financial status (major "life events"), review how your new circumstances will affect your overall financial planning.

☐ ☐ 4. Discuss money matters openly and regularly with your spouse.

☐ ☐ 5. Create a personal record-keeping system that is comprehensive enough to be useful yet simple enough that you will use it.

☐ ☐ 6. Prepare a statement of personal assets and liabilities periodically to measure your financial planning progress.

☐ ☐ 7. Select your financial advisers with care, and be aware of any potential conflicts of interest that they might have.

☐ ☐ 8. If you are not satisfied with a financial adviser, don't hesitate to make a change.

☐ ☐ 9. Be particularly careful in selecting a financial planner. Be sure he or she has the qualifications necessary to meet your needs.

*Needs   Okay or
Action   Not Applicable*

☐   ☐   10. Of the ten common mistakes that indepen-
                             dent businesspeople make (discussed at the end
                             of this chapter), list those that represent potential
                             problems in your situation:

                             . . . .
                             . . . .
                             . . . .
                             . . . .
                             . . . .
                             . . . .

Comments: . . . .
. . . .
. . . .
. . . .
. . . .
. . . .

Financial Planning and Record-Keeping "To Do" List: . . . .
. . . .
. . . .
. . . .
. . . .
. . . .

2

Reducing Personal Risk with Insurance

———

You may be tempted to skip this chapter because there is nothing more boring than insurance. But if you are so inclined, you might as well skip the rest of the book; unless you have adequate insurance coverage, there is no sense in doing the more exciting things associated with personal financial planning, such as investing and planning for a financially comfortable retirement. Independent businesspeople understand and try to reduce risk in their businesses. Why, then, do they sometimes assume unnecessary personal risk by being underinsured or uninsured? I can assure you that a single gap in your insurance coverage could jeopardize a lifetime's worth of sacrifice and savings. So adequate insurance coverage is every bit as important in planning for your financial security as the other, more appealing, personal financial matters.

AVOIDING MISTAKES IN INSURANCE COVERAGE

Most people understand the need for health insurance, life insurance, homeowner's insurance, and automobile insurance, yet they often leave gaps in their coverage that could prove to be very costly. Although many are aware of how devastating a loss of assets or earning power can be to themselves and their families, only a few take well-thought-out, informed steps to insure against that possibility. While your insurance agent can be indispensable in helping you obtain and maintain adequate coverage, you probably need to take more control over the process.

Insurance products are becoming increasingly sophisticated and differentiated. While the level of confusion surrounding insurance is getting worse, many of the new insurance products on the market are better.

To avoid mistakes in securing adequate insurance coverage, you must keep the following in mind:

Cover all gaps. You and your insurance agent must be sure that all foreseeable areas of risk are covered with insurance. The most common gaps in coverage are: lack of an umbrella liability policy (often called "extended liability insurance"); inadequate long-term disability coverage (a particular problem for self-employed professionals and small business owners); and insufficient coverage on valuable personal possessions such as jewelry and silverware.

Obtain the correct policy coverage. Each policy that you need to purchase, either through your business or personally, must be evaluated in detail so that you are assured of receiving the coverage you need. As discussed later in this chapter, policies can vary significantly in the extent of their coverage. This does not necessarily mean you need to purchase the most comprehensive policy, but you do need to assure that the coverage meets your needs. Policy limits are also an important consideration. For example, an otherwise excellent health policy might have a major medical cap that is too low.

Adjust coverage to meet your changing needs. Even though you may have adequate coverage now, your needs will undoubtedly change in the future. Therefore, you need to review the adequacy of your insurance coverage at least annually, and if there is an obvious change in your status—for example, the birth of a child or a substantial increase in your income—you need an immediate review.

Minimize the cost of insurance. Many segments of the insurance industry are intensely competitive, and premiums for similar policy coverage can vary dramatically. You may well be able to

---

Why do they call it "life" insurance when you have to die in order to collect on the policy?

achieve significant savings with careful shopping and selection of policy features. "Cheaper" does not necessarily mean "better," but studies have shown that many people pay far more for their insurance coverage than they need to.

While securing the right kind of insurance coverage does not vary significantly from occupation to occupation, many independent businesspeople have unique needs that must be addressed in order to assure that their coverage is comprehensive.

■ Independent businesspeople who have employees often cannot afford to provide much insurance coverage through the company. Therefore, they will have to obtain adequate health, disability, and life insurance from other sources. Unfortunately, the high cost of this insurance discourages many self-employed people from obtaining adequate coverage.

■ Many self-employed people have insufficient disability income insurance coverage. Whether it is purchased on a group basis through your business or individually, this coverage is expensive. Moreover, any group coverage you provide for yourself and, if applicable, for your employees may lack the features and extent of coverage that are necessary to be fully protected.

■ Small business owners and self-employed professionals often fail to obtain sufficient life insurance to provide adequately for their dependents as well as for the orderly disposition or continuation of the business.

■ High-income professionals often fail to obtain enough life insurance to enable their dependents to sustain a standard of living equivalent to the living standard when the insured was alive.

■ Because of their wealth and prominence in the community, many self-employed professionals and small business owners need higher limits of insurance coverage than might otherwise be necessary. For example, they should have high-limit umbrella liability insurance because, sadly, they represent attractive targets for personal liability lawsuits.

■ Because of the demands on their time, many independent businesspeople rely too heavily on an insurance agent or financial adviser to evaluate and obtain insurance coverage. This can result not only in securing inappropriate coverage but also in paying too much for it.

The following sections provide some guidance on selecting appropriate and comprehensive insurance. Table 2 summarizes the major areas of insurance coverage.

T A B L E   2

Important Areas of Insurance Coverage

TYPE OF INSURANCE	DESCRIPTION/FEATURES
Health Insurance	Protects you from both the out-of-pocket costs of health care and large cash outflows during major illness.
Homeowner's Insurance	Property, such as a home, other structures, personal property, and general contents of the dwelling are insured against theft or destruction; protects against the possibility of cash outflows for replacement of these assets.
Renter's Insurance	Protects the personal possessions of the tenant.
Automobile Insurance	Protects you from large cash outflows for damages resulting from automobile accident or theft.
Personal Liability Insurance	Protects you from having personal assets or future earnings forfeited as a result of a personal liability suit. Provides additional protection on top of homeowner's and automobile liability coverage.
Disability Insurance	Replaces part or most of your income (and, in the case of small business owners, can replace business overhead) in the event of disability.
Life Insurance	Replaces part or most of your business income in the event of your death and covers nonrecurring expenses of your dependents during a readjustment period after death.

TYPE OF INSURANCE	DESCRIPTION/FEATURES
Professional Liability	Protects you from claims arising out of professional acts or omissions. Depending on the nature of your business or profession, you may need professional liability, errors and omissions, and/or product liability insurance.

LIFE INSURANCE

Although the primary goal of life insurance is to provide adequate resources for the deceased's dependents, it can also provide for other postmortem financial needs, including paying estate taxes and assuring that your business will continue to operate or can be sold or liquidated in an orderly fashion. If you are confused about the complexities involved in selecting life insurance, you are not alone. The life insurance industry seems to thrive on obfuscation.

ESTIMATING YOUR LIFE INSURANCE NEEDS

Figuring out how much life insurance you need is no easy task. Most of us are either underinsured or overinsured. Of course, the people who need a lot of life insurance are those with dependent children. But children are not necessarily the only dependents you might have. For example, "dinks," or dual in-come couples with no kids, may need more life insurance than they think if, as is often the case, they are enjoying a life-style so profligate that a surviving spouse would be financially crippled by the other's demise. You probably know some dinks—they often have a huge mortgage, ever-present car loans, and no savings.

If you are concerned about providing for dependents, one way to estimate your insurance needs is to look at two extremes—a maximum and a minimum. First, figure out how much insur-ance it would take to provide for all of your dependents' financial needs. This would typically include payment of readjustment expenses during the period immediately after your demise, plus paying off your outstanding debts, plus income for your spouse throughout his or her lifetime. Obviously, if you buy enough insurance to cover all expenses, your spouse will undoubtedly be the most financially desirable widow or widower in town. So the other extreme you need to estimate is a minimum amount that will allow your family a few years to become self-sufficient after your death. This may be an amount equivalent to four or five years of your net income—enough to allow your family some time to get back on a firm economic footing. If you can estimate the extremes, you can then make a sensible decision as to an amount appropriate for you and your dependents. The following Life Insurance Needs Work Sheet will help you make this decision.

Your life insurance needs typically decline as you age. In order to plan the kind of insurance you need, you should estimate not only how much coverage you need now but also how much you expect to need in the future. Finally, don't rely too much on someone else's estimate of your life insurance requirements. The insurance industry loves to run projections for potential policy-holders, and these projections can be very helpful. But, as we all understand, the insurance company estimates are not likely to err on the low side when it comes to estimating how much life insurance you need.

Because you have your own business or are a self-employed professional, you may need to consider the use of life insurance to assure an orderly disposition of your business as well as to assure that your survivors are compensated adequately for your business. An example of such an arrangement is a "buy–sell agreement," which is usually funded with life insurance policies. Working out the details of these arrangements requires the combined expertise of your attorney, accountant, and insurance adviser.

Many independent businesspeople manage to amass large estates. Even though you may not now be able to envision accumulating an estate that would incur substantial estate taxes, you may eventually be in that position. Therefore, you should at least consider using life insurance to help pay off your estate taxes when the time comes, because if your estate lacks sufficient cash or assets that are readily convertible into cash, your survivors may have to liquidate valuable and productive assets to pay death taxes and administrative expenses. Careful planning is necessary, of course. So-called split-dollar life insurance may be worth considering. Split-dollar insurance is a method of purchasing whole life insurance through your company, where the cost of the premiums as well as the ultimate payment of benefits are split between your comapny and the beneficiary. Depending on your particular circumstances, there may be advantages to both your company and you personally from such arrangements. On the other hand, life insurance that the business buys on your behalf may, in some circumstances, not be the best way to hold a life insurance policy. Your advisers may recommend establishing an "irrevocable life insurance trust" as the best way to provide estate liquidity. If you are married with children, you should probably consider a so-called second-to-die life insurance policy. This policy names you and your spouse as joint insureds and pays the death benefit only at the death of the second spouse. Second-to-die policies offer lower premiums and make sense in many instances, particularly when both spouses and other family members are active in the business, because no federal estate tax is incurred on the death of the first spouse owing to the unlimited marital deduction.

LIFE INSURANCE NEEDS WORK SHEET

The following work sheet can be used to estimate your life insurance needs. If you enter amounts for each category of need, the resulting estimate should be viewed as a *maximum* amount of insurance that will meet all foreseeable needs of your survivors. (*Note:* All amounts should be expressed in terms of current dollars.)

EXPENSES

1. Final expenses (one-time expenses incurred by your death)
   a. Final illness (medical costs will probably exceed health insurance deductibles and coinsurance, so assume you will have to fund at least those amounts) $............
   b. Burial/funeral costs ....
   c. Probate costs (if unsure, assume 4 percent of assets passing through the probate process) ....
   d. Federal estate taxes (for most estates over $600,000 willed to someone other than spouse) ....
   e. State inheritance taxes (varies by state) ....
   f. Legal fees, estate administration ....
   g. Other ....
   h. Total final expenses $............

2. Outstanding debt (to be paid off at your death)
   a. Credit card/consumer debt   ....
   b. Car   ....
   c. Mortgage (if it's to be paid off at your death; otherwise, include payments in life income)   ....
   d. Other   ....
   e. Total outstanding debt $...........

3. Readjustment expenses (to cover the transition period of immediate crisis)
   a. Child care   ....
   b. Additional homemaking help   ....
   c. Vocational counseling/educational training (for a nonworking or underemployed spouse who expects to seek paid employment)   ....
   d. Costs of continuing business and/or disposing of business interests in an orderly fashion (if business does not already provide sufficient life insurance coverage)   ....
   e. Other   ....
   f. Total readjustment expenses $...........

4. Dependency expenses (until all children are self-supporting)
   a. Estimate your household's current annual expenditures   ....
   b. To remove the deceased person's expenses, multiply this figure by:
      .70 for a surviving family of one
      .74 for a surviving family of two
      .78 for a surviving family of three
      .80 for a surviving family of four
      .82 for a surviving family of five
      $..... (Line 4a) × ..... (factor) = ...
   c. Deduct spouse's estimated annual income from employment   (.......)
   d. Equals current annual expenses to be covered by currently owned assets and insurance   ....
   e. To determine approximate total dependency expenses required, multiply by number of years until youngest child becomes self-supporting:
      $..... (Line 4b) x ..... (years) = ...
   f. If support for dependent parent(s) is to be provided, multiply annual support by the number of years such support is expected to continue: $....... × ..... (years) = ...

    g. Total dependency expenses (add Lines 4e
       and 4f) $...........

5. Education expenses
    a. Annual private school tuition in
       current dollars (if desired)   ....
    b. Multiply by number of years and children
       left to attend:
       $....... (Line 5a) × ..... (years) = ...
    c. Annual college costs in current
       dollars   ....
    d. Multiply by number of years and children
       left to attend:
       $....... (Line 5c) × ..... (years) = ...
    e. Total education expenses (add Lines 5b
       and 5d) $...........

6. Life income (for the surviving spouse after the children are all
self-supporting)
    a. Annual amount desired (in current
       dollars)   ....
    b. Deduct spouse's estimated annual
       income from employment   (.......)
    c. Equals annual expenses to be covered by
       currently owned assets and insurance   ....
    d. Multiply by number of years between when the youngest
       child becomes self-supporting and the surviving spouse
       begins receiving Social Security benefits and other
       retirement income, if any:
       $....... (Line 6c) × ..... (years) = $...........

7. Retirement income for surviving spouse
    a. Annual amount desired in current dollars
       (less Social Security and any pension
       income)   ....
    b. Multiply by number of years of life expectancy after
       retirement begins:
       $....... (Line 7a) × ..... (years) = $...........

8. Total funds needed to cover expenses:
(add Lines 1h, 2e, 3f, 4g, 5e, 6d, and 7b) $...........

ASSETS CURRENTLY AVAILABLE TO SUPPORT FAMILY
      Proceeds from life insurance already owned $...........
      Cash and savings   ....
      Equity in real estate (if survivors will sell)   ....
      Securities   ....
      IRA and Keogh, and/or other pension plans   ....
      Company savings plans   ....
      Other sources   ....
9.   Total assets $...........

ADDITIONAL LIFE INSURANCE REQUIRED
10. Subtract available assets (Line 9) from total funds needed to
cover expenses (Line 8).
This shortfall represents the estimated amount that must be
covered through life insurance. $............

WHAT KIND OF LIFE INSURANCE POLICIES ARE RIGHT FOR YOU?

Once you have an idea of how much life insurance you need,
you then must try to figure out the best kind of coverage to
obtain, if any, in addition to the coverage you undoubtedly already have. Table 3 summarizes the various types of life insurance products.

T A B L E   3

Life Insurance Policy Alternatives

TYPE OF POLICY	DESCRIPTION/FEATURES
Term	*Term* insurance only provides death protection. A term policy does not build a cash value. If the insured discontinues insurance premiums payments, the coverage simply lapses after a specific grace period. This is the cheapest form of immediate insurance protection. There are many kinds of term insurance. Term insurance premiums increase with age for the same amount of coverage, although most people's life insurance requirements decrease with age. A *renewable term* policy covers the insured for a fixed period of years or until a specified age. With renewable term, the insured may usually renew the policy each year without a medical examination. *Decreasing term* provides constant premiums over time with a declining amount of death protection.
Whole Life	Also called *straight* or *ordinary life*. Requires level premium payments over

TYPE OF POLICY	DESCRIPTION/FEATURES
	the lifetime of the insured and provides cash value that increases slowly in the early years and more rapidly in the later years of the policy. The rate of increase in the cash value is predetermined. A number of variations are also available. Under a *limited payment life* policy, premium payments remain level up to a certain age and then cease. *Adjustable life* plans allow the insured to change both the premium payments and the face amount of the policy as needs and income vary.
Universal Life	*Universal life* permits flexible premium payments. The cash value portion of the policy is deposited into an interest-bearing account that is usually tied to a predetermined index. Most universal policies allow the insured to increase the death protection, although another medical examination may be required. Universal life insurance policies have been designed to provide considerable flexibility to the amount of coverage and the amount of premium.
Variable Life	The cash value portion of *variable life* is invested in one or more stock, bond, and money market funds of the policyholder's choosing. Therefore, the cash value will fluctuate based on the performance of these separate investment accounts.
Single Premium Whole Life	*Single premium* policies are paid up in one or very few installments. The emphasis in these policies is on investment, not insurance. Like other cash-value policies, the cash values build up tax free.

CASH VALUE OR TERM?

Life insurance is a commodity item in an intensely competitive industry. While most life insurance is sold, not purchased, you may benefit from comparison shopping for the lowest-priced policy that meets your needs. Whether term insurance or cash value is preferable is, has been, and always will be the subject of intense debate. Most financial planning matters need not be reduced to an either/or decision. And this can be said of the term-versus-cash-value insurance dilemma. The decision depends on your individual circumstance, but many self-employed professionals and small business owners who enjoy a high income and require considerable life insurance may benefit from a combination of term insurance and *some* cash value insurance. You should not attempt to meet all your life insurance needs through cash value coverage because of the high premiums associated with cash value insurance. Some people have too much cash value insurance. While the tax deferral features are certainly attractive, the generally high commissions and fees associated with these policies drag down returns in comparison with returns that can be garnered on other investments.

If you find you need more term insurance, there are several sources of low-cost coverage you should investigate. First, you may be able to obtain inexpensive group coverage through your own business. The rates are usually very attractive. Another source of low-cost insurance coverage is through professional groups and associations. Numerous associations for self-employed professionals and small business owners offer very attractive rates to their members. Coverage is also available to spouses through these group insurance programs.

You may be unhappy with a cash value policy you have already purchased, probably because you didn't understand it when it was sold to you. On reflection, you realize it is an expensive way to buy life insurance protection, and the cash value side of the policy isn't such a hot investment. Should you cash the policy in? Probably not, particularly if you've been paying premiums on it for a number of years, because the cash value increase will become more attractive as the policy "ages." Since most of your initial premiums went to pay commissions and other fees, you probably shouldn't cash in a relatively new policy either.

If I bought the amount of life insurance my agent tells me I need, my wife would not only be able to buy the nicest plot in the town cemetery to bury me; she'd also be able to buy the whole town.

ADDITIONAL TIPS FOR SECURING APPROPRIATE LIFE COVERAGE

Make sure your term insurance policies are *renewable,* which guarantees you will be able to renew your policy for an additional term, albeit at a higher annual premium. Incidentally, a lender may encourage you to purchase *decreasing term* when you take out a mortgage, automobile, or other installment loan. The amount of insurance coverage decreases over time as your outstanding loan balance decreases. If you think decreasing term is a good idea for a large loan, you're probably better off shopping around for coverage since the policies offered by lending institutions are usually expensive—as much as twenty times more expensive than comparable group policies!

If you are turned down for life insurance owing to a health condition, don't despair. A good agent will find coverage for you, and you'll probably be surprised at how little additional premium is required, if any. If your agent can't help you, some insurance agencies have specialists in substandard risks. You also might be able to find a nonmedical group policy.

Affluent professionals and small business owners must be particularly careful when specifying policy owners and beneficiaries. These designations can have significant estate planning implications, and the earlier you resolve these matters, the better. Don't rely on your agent to advise you; use a good estate planning attorney instead. And remember, while the proceeds of your life insurance policy are not subject to income taxes (the agents love to tell you this), they may be subject to estate taxes (funny, they don't tell you this). There are ways around this, but like all other sophisticated estate planning techniques, they require considerable legal expertise.

MEDICAL INSURANCE

Everyone understands the importance of adequate and continuous medical insurance. But you do need to be aware that policies vary in what they do and do not cover. Since you are self-employed, you are painfully aware of the rapidly escalating cost of medical insurance. Unless you have a spouse whose employer offers medical coverage, you are probably going to be required either to pay more for coverage or accept reduced coverage. Either way, you must plan carefully to meet all foreseeable medical expenses, particularly if they are going to come out of your own pocket. If your major medical policy has an upper limit of coverage that makes you uncomfortable, you may want to consider purchasing an excess major medical policy separately. This coverage is relatively inexpensive.

You are probably becoming aware of the difficulty experienced by small businesses in obtaining adequate medical coverage at a reasonable cost. As with any of the other insurance coverage areas, you or your insurance adviser will benefit from investigating the policies offered by several carriers. Before purchasing an individual policy, you should consider acquiring group medical insurance coverage, which is usually available at more attractive group rates. Alternatively, you may want to consider an individually purchased major medical policy with a high deductible if you can afford the amount of the deductible comfortably.

A few other health insurance considerations may also apply to you.

■ Be sure your children always have sufficient medical coverage even if they have left the nest and are on their own. If your children are in college, be sure your policy covers them adequately, and if not, don't expect the group plan offered by your child's college to be adequate.

■ If your parents are retired, check with them to make sure they have Medicare Gap insurance to supplement Medicare. Also, make sure they don't fall prey to unscrupulous agents who attempt to sell them either duplicative policies or narrowly defined insurance policies, such as cancer insurance.

■ If you are traveling overseas, make sure your medical insurance carrier will provide coverage. Most do. Medicare, however, does not provide any coverage outside the United States (except in Canada and Mexico under very limited circumstances). Therefore, Medicare-eligible travelers should purchase a medical policy that will cover them during their sojourn aboard. These low-cost policies are available through travel agencies.

DISABILITY INSURANCE

Although the insurance industry seems most concerned about selling life insurance, you are far more likely to suffer from a long-term disability during your working years than you are to die. The effect of the disability of a business owner can be devastating. Long-term disability coverage is, therefore, essen-

> It's okay not to have any health insurance, just don't get sick.

tial. Yet many independent businesspeople either lack disability coverage altogether or have insufficient coverage. Since you are self-employed, it is particularly crucial for you to have comprehensive and sufficient disability insurance.

DETERMINING HOW MUCH YOU NEED

Many people whose businesses provide long-term disability coverage think this coverage is sufficient. That may or may not be the case. A short-term disability resulting from, say, a heart attack, arthritis, or accident can seriously disrupt one's financial life. A long-term disability is certain to be financially, emotionally, and professionally traumatic. With adequate disability insurance coverage you can at least minimize your financial loss. The following work sheet will allow you to estimate approximately how much additional disability insurance coverage you need.

As a business owner, you must also be concerned about the effects of your disability on the continuation of your business.

DISABILITY INCOME NEEDS WORK SHEET

Resources needed:
1. Total annual family living expenses $........
2. Subtract annual expenses that go away if you became disabled, such as taxes (disability benefits may be partly or fully tax free), work-related expenses, entertainment, and travel. (.......)
3. Adjusted annual family living expenses
    (subtract line 2 from line 1)   ....
Resources available:
4. Annual income from savings and investments
    (dividends and interest)   ....
5. Annual income from spouse's job   ....
6. Annual disability benefits provided by your company's policy   ....
7. Annual disability benefits provided by other disability policies
    currently owned   ....
8. Total available resources
    (add lines 4, 5, 6, and 7)   ....
9. Additional resources needed either from liquidating assets or
    additional disability insurance (subtract line 8 from line 3) $........

Disability of a business owner can have a devastating impact on a business. Therefore, you should consider obtaining, in addition to disability coverage to provide for lost earnings, "business overhead insurance." During your disability this will help cover business expenses that will be necessary during its continuation. Business overhead insurance in general is cheaper than disability income insurance.

One other matter that bears on your estimate of the amount of disability insurance you need is the taxability of benefits. Disability income is taxable if payments are attributable to employer contributions to a disability plan. Benefits are excludable from income if you pay the premiums yourself rather than have your corporation pay for them. Therefore, if you are incorporated, you may want to consider paying your own disability insurance premium (and your spouse's, if applicable) rather than having your corporation make them. Then, if you ever become disabled, you will be able to receive the disability payments tax free.

WHERE TO OBTAIN COVERAGE

Group disability coverage varies widely in policy limits and features. Some are quite good, but others are unsatisfactory. If you have obtained coverage for yourself and, if applicable, your employees, you understand why so many group disability policies offer limited benefits. Good disability insurance is expensive, even on a group basis. Yet group coverage is considerably cheaper than individually purchased policies. If you haven't already, you should consider obtaining group disability insurance through your business, although you will have to weigh the cost of providing this coverage for your employees against the company's ability to afford it. Alternatively—or if you need more coverage than you obtained through your business—you should investigate the lower-cost disability insurance provided by many professional groups and associations.

Even though you may have obtained group disability insurance through your business, you should still consider individually purchased coverage as well, because many of the desirable policy features discussed below probably won't be available in a group policy. Disability insurance is nothing to scrimp on. You are seven times more likely to become disabled than you are to die before you retire. You may end up paying several hundred dollars, or even more than $1,000 per year, to obtain good coverage. I think it is money well spent, unless, of course, you are lucky enough to be financially independent already. If you have any health problems, disability insurance will be difficult to obtain at good rates, but diligent shopping by an agent willing to go to bat for you should get the coverage you need. Incidentally, the aggregate amount of disability coverage you can receive from all policies, group and individual, generally cannot exceed 80 percent of your earned income and possibly somewhat less.

IMPORTANT POLICY FEATURES

Disability policies have a mind-boggling number of features. In addition to being guaranteed renewable and noncancellable, the following options and features are well worth considering if you need to obtain more disability insurance. You might also check the policy features on insurance you already have, both group and individual, against the following. It should help you assess the quality of your existing policies.

Definition of "disability." The best policies will continue disability payments so long as the insured suffers a loss of income. The next level makes payments as long as the insured is unable to perform the "usual and customary" duties of the insured's occupation. Some policies tighten the requirements, defining disability as the inability to perform *all* the duties of the insured's occupation. This distinction is crucial, for example, in the case of a self-employed engineer whose income was more than $100,000 a year but who earns $45,000 as a consultant because of a crippling illness. Under the more stringent definition, he or she would not be entitled to disability payments. Other policies regard disability as the inability to perform any job. You should also check on the policy provisions regarding payments for rehabilitation. Some are very generous, and this is to your advantage, of course.

Period of coverage. All long-term disability policies have a waiting period between the onset of disability and the date the payments begin. If you are purchasing a policy, lengthening the waiting period will reduce the premium, sometimes considerably. Be sure to get quotes on longer waiting periods—three months, six months, and one year. Benefits should always be payable until age 65, when retirement benefits will presumably kick in.

It's okay not to have enough disability insurance, just don't become disabled.

Cost-of-living adjustments. COLAs are an expensive option yet are well worth considering. Most policies pay a fixed monthly benefit as long as you are disabled. The benefit may seem satisfactory now, but would it be ten or twenty years hence if you become permanently disabled?

PROPERTY INSURANCE

Most people have insurance on their home(s) and automobile(s). Surprisingly, fewer than one-quarter of renters have renter's insurance, although every renter should. Property insurance is pretty straightforward, but many people fail to understand the limitations of the standard property insurance policy. So you need to focus on the commonly overlooked areas of risk, to assure that you don't have any unpleasant surprises if and when you suffer a loss.

TOTING UP YOUR WORLDLY GOODS

If you come home from work next week and find the fire department shoveling what's left of your home into the back of a truck, could you give your insurer a detailed list of your personal property? If you're like most people, you couldn't even prepare a very complete list of the contents of your wallet, much less the contents of your home. You need to take an inventory of your household possessions. (And you might as well make a list of your wallet contents, too.) A household inventory involves recording pertinent information on your possessions, and the more valuable the possession, the more detailed the information. You can do this in writing or by speaking into a tape recorder. Also, take a lot of photographs of your possessions. If you have extensive personal property, you can hire a bonded videotaping service to do the dirty work. Store the inventory information at the office or in your safe-deposit box. Next time you go to the safe-deposit box, make a list of its contents, too. When you acquire additional possessions, put the receipts in with your inventory. If you ever suffer a loss, you'll be very glad you have an up-to-date household inventory. Of course, you should also take an inventory of the assets held by your business, whether they are located in your home or at your place of business.

Assuring complete coverage. Even if you select comprehensive basic homeowner's and auto policies, you probably haven't covered all of the risks that you want to protect against. You probably need some "optional extras" to obtain the coverage you need.

Replacement cost coverage. Homeowner's insurance should cover 80 to 100 percent of the replacement value of the home including any improvements that have been made, allowing for annual inflation. The basic insurance coverage usually specifies actual cash value or market value. Using these estimates can lead to underinsurance, however, since repair costs rise faster than the market value of the house. Make sure your policy has sufficient coverage to pay for the total replacement of your home.

Replacement cost coverage on the contents of the house or, in the case of a tenant, the apartment, is usually an extremely valuable option as well. Otherwise, you will be paid actual cash (i.e., depreciated) value for any losses. Not only does this often lead to disputes with the carrier, it also can result in your having to pay a lot of money out of your own pocket to replace the lost or damaged items. Replacement cost coverage on personal property is normally available as a separate policy rider.

Floater policies. Basic homeowner's and renter's policies impose severe limits on the amount they will pay for valuables. Therefore, your valuables should be professionally appraised and covered under a floater. A floater provides a specific amount of insurance for each object on an itemized basis, guaranteeing full replacement value and eliminating deductibles. Floaters should provide "all-risk" coverage; in other words, they will pay no matter what happens to the valuable, even if you unwittingly lose it. Valuables should be reappraised every few years, and floater coverage should be adjusted accordingly. In lieu of a floater policy, you might be able to increase the blanket valuables coverage on your homeowner's or renter's policy from the standard $1,000 to a higher level.

If you store any valuables in a safe-deposit box, you should also obtain a floater that covers these items since banks rarely insure against loss from safe-deposit boxes.

HOME OFFICE RIDER

If you operate your business out of your home, beware. Homeowner's insurance does not cover property damage related to the operation of a full- or part-time business in the home. For example, a personal computer within the home that is used primarily for business is not covered. With some exceptions, home office coverage is available as a rider to the basic policy. If a home office rider is not sufficient, a home office policy, available separately, should be obtained.

AUTOMOBILE INSURANCE

Many people pay more for car insurance than they need to. When your policy comes up for renewal, don't just continue the same coverage. Look for ways to save. Higher deductibles, driving a more conservative car, and dropping expensive policy options can result in lower premiums.

PERSONAL LIABILITY INSURANCE

Extended personal liability insurance, also called umbrella insurance, is one of the most often overlooked gaps in insurance coverage. If you don't have this coverage, you are jeopardizing assets you currently own and perhaps even some of your future earnings. Spurred on by higher and higher awards in court actions, injured parties, real or fancied, have become more willing to press claims against others for individual acts. If the defendant's assets are insufficient to pay the settlement, the court may award the plaintiff a portion of the defendant's future earnings. I once met a self-employed surgeon who told me he had been paying a fortune for professional liability insurance, but who wasn't aware of the need for umbrella coverage until he rear-ended a car driven by a person who, according to the doctor, made his living jamming on his brakes in front of expensive cars. The physician ended up losing a lot of assets and a portion of his future earnings.

Umbrella policies typically protect you and your family (including children away at college and pets) from claims arising out of your nonprofessional activities, including legal defense costs. However, it is important to understand the exclusions written into the umbrella policy.

This coverage is realtively inexpensive; annual premiums for $1 million in liability insurance generally are between $100 and $200. If you are a financially successful independent businessperson, $1 million in personal liability coverage is probably too little in this litigious age. Many insurance experts suggest that $2 million or even more is desirable. Umbrella insurance is coordinated with your automobile and homeowner's/renter's insurance policies, so you may have to increase the liability limits on these policies before qualifying for the umbrella. Umbrella insurance is crucial for everyone.

PROFESSIONAL AND BUSINESS LIABILITY INSURANCE

Umbrella insurance does not cover a liability arising out of any job-related activities. While this is not a chapter on business insurance, I need to remind you to be sure to obtain the necessary professional or business (errors and omissions or product liability, for example) liability insurance. This insurance is on the one hand essential and, on the other hand, becoming very expensive for some professions and businesses. If you are uncertain about either the need for this important coverage or where to obtain it, check with an insurance professional who is experienced in providing professional liability coverage, or check with your trade association.

THE CARE AND FEEDING OF INSURANCE AGENTS

A good insurance professional can be a great help in assuring that you are insured adequately and economically. The personal and business insurance needs of most small business owners and self-employed professionals are particularly complex, and therefore the expertise of competent insurance representatives is required. The good ones know their business and know your circumstances. Make them earn their commissions. I'm often asked how you can tell a good agent from a mediocre one. A good agent will review your coverage annually, and will not simply use that occasion just to try to sell annuities, mutual funds, or cash value life insurance. A good agent will also urge you to obtain coverage essential to your well-being even if it doesn't generate much commission. For example, if you haven't been told about the importance of umbrella liability insurance, you probably need a new agent.

> Don't leave home without your umbrella (insurance).

Hopefully, you understand what it takes to be insured adequately. You can summarize your insurance status on the Insurance Coverage Checkup, and the Insurance Action Plan that follows can, with periodic reviews, keep you alert to insurance concerns that require your attention. You might be thinking that with all of the insurance you need, you won't have any money left over. Don't worry. The next chapter will show you how to control your spending and get your debt under control so you not only can afford to pay your insurance premiums, but also can save money so that you can get rich—sensibly.

INSURANCE COVERAGE CHECKUP
Date: _____

Type of Insurance	Source of Coverage	Check One		
		Adequate	Additional or improved necessary	Coverage not needed
Life	_____	☐	☐	☐
Medical	_____	☐	☐	☐
Disability	_____	☐	☐	☐
Homeowner's/ Renter's	_____	☐	☐	☐
Automobile	_____	☐	☐	☐
Personal liability (umbrella)	_____	☐	☐	☐
Professional or business liability	_____	☐	☐	☐

Comments _____
_____
_____
_____
_____

INSURANCE ACTION PLAN

CURRENT STATUS

Needs   *Okay or*
Action   *Not Applicable*

☐   ☐   1. Review all your insurance coverage at least annually. Your insurance agent should orchestrate this review.

☐   ☐   2. Prepare your own estimate of your life insurance needs. Don't rely on others to do it for you.

☐   ☐   3. Be sure you or your agent obtains quotations from several companies before purchasing any life insurance.

☐   ☐   4. If you need term insurance, be sure to investigate group coverage that can be purchased through your business or through professional groups and associations.

☐   ☐   5. If you have an estate that is likely to be near or in excess of $1 million, check with an estate planning attorney to assure that you have designated appropriate life insurance policy owners and beneficiaries.

☐   ☐   6. Be sure that all family members, including parents and children who are out of the nest, have adequate and continuous health insurance.

☐   ☐   7. Evaluate the sufficiency of the amount and the policy provisions of all disability insurance policies currently owned.

☐   ☐   8. If necessary, obtain additional disability coverage. Look for group coverage that can be purchased through your business, or individually purchased policies with desirable features.

☐   ☐   9. Take an inventory of your household possessions.

☐   ☐   10. Evaluate the adequacy of your homeowner's or renter's insurance and add to the coverage if you find any areas that are not fully insured.

☐   ☐   11. If you operate your business out of your home, be sure to obtain adequate business insurance through your homeowner's/renter's policy or through a separate policy.

☐   ☐   12. If your profession or business warrants it, obtain professional or business liability coverage.

☐   ☐   13. Obtain an extended personal liability (umbrella) policy if you haven't already.

☐   ☐   14. Consider increasing the amount of umbrella coverage if you now have only $1 million.

☐   ☐   15. Your insurance agent should be competent and responsive. If not, make a change.

3

Maximizing Your Capital by Minimizing Your Spending and Borrowing

BUSINESS OWNERS MUST CONTROL THEIR SPENDING AND BORROWING

A lot of people envy small business owners and self-employed professionals. They envy the freedom you enjoy as well as the ability to control your own destiny. They envy you because you are insulated from layoffs and early retirement incentive (coercion) plans. They wouldn't envy you as much if they understood the "downside" of business ownership—the long hours, the ever-present uncertainty, and the financial risk. While this book deals with your *personal* finances, it is often difficult to separate your business's finances from your personal finances.

Most self-employed businesspeople must exercise particular care in their personal spending and borrowing. They should always be prepared for a downturn in their business, which may require dipping into personal resources to meet business expenses or, perhaps, to sustain the business. In my experience, I have found that business owners who are always looking over their shoulders expecting, and preparing for, the worst are best able to weather the almost inevitable periodic business downturn.

EXAMPLE: Several years ago I worked with a small business owner who, after many years of hard work, began to reap the fruits of his labor. His cyclical manufacturing business had been flying high for a couple of years, and it almost became necessary to add a *third* shift. He began to reward his hard work, first with a new, custom-built home, then with a couple of expensive cars, then a second home. Shortly thereafter, the inevitable downturn hit. He had to reduce prices, and his more formidable competitors were undercutting him. In less than a year, his business was bankrupt, although there is a happy ending to the story. Now chastened, this indomitable entrepreneur has started up again on a smaller scale. The fancy life-style is gone, and in its place is, as he says, "enough money in my personal bank account to sustain my business for a year with no sales."

Self-employed professionals and small business owners have unique circumstances that should influence their spending and borrowing habits.

■ As illustrated in the above example, the always possible prospect of a declining income requires the independent businessperson to set aside sufficient personal resources to weather the storm. In the worst situation, they may have to finance not only living expenses but also business overhead expenses.
■ Self-employed professionals and small business owners must strive to develop and maintain a good credit standing so that they can access borrowing, if necessary, to tide them over a lean period. On the other hand, they must resist the temptation to overextend themselves personally in order to finance a declining business.
■ The relatively high income enjoyed by many self-employed professionals and small business owners makes it easy to establish a very comfortable, if not lavish, life-style. All the ingredients are there—income, access to credit, and visibility in the community. Sadly, as many independent businesspeople have found out, a life-style that relies on a continuing stream of high income cannot always be sustained.

Even if your borrowing and spending are in reasonably good shape, there is always some room for improvement. So read on.

HOW TO SAVE MONEY: THE SECRET FORMULA REVEALED

The shortest routes to wealth are to marry it or inherit it. If neither applies to you, there is only one remaining alternative—to accumulate it yourself. If you're lucky, your business may provide you with the wealth you need to achieve financial security and then some. But you must be realistic in assessing the probability that this will come true. Most businesses do not create enough resources in and of themselves to provide financial security. Therefore, just like salaried people, you must accumulate investments outside of the business. If so, I'll let you in on a secret—a surefire, can't-fail way to accumulate wealth: Spend less than you earn. I guess this must be a secret because so few people do it. Why does this tautological concept elude so many of us? It is simply too easy to spend money. Our society rewards spending. People love to brag about their expensive automobiles and other possessions. How often do you hear people brag about the amount of money they save? Never, because if they did, they would be branded as social misfits. We all would like to save, and we all know we need to save or to save more, but living beneath our means is tough, particularly for many small business owners who have spent years living on a subsistence basis while building up their businesses.

How much should you save? At least 10 percent of your *gross* income, although 15 to 20 percent is, of course, better. While you may count any contributions you make to your company's retirement plan, you should also be saving some money outside the retirement plan. If you think I'm asking you to save too much, take a glance at Chapter 7, which covers retirement planning. It helps you estimate how much you will need to save (amass, really) by the time you retire. A high rate of savings, particularly in years of high income, may be particularly important for independent businesspeople because of the uncertainty as to the level of future income inherent in small business ownership.

If you are having difficulty saving or would like to save more, you need to identify areas where you can reduce your spending, then find a way to save the money as painlessly as possible.

PUTTING YOUR LIVING EXPENSES ON A STRICT BUDGET

Most people aren't too anxious to summarize how they spend their income because they know they aren't going to like what they see. But you really should prepare a budget from time to time. Your business can't operate effectively and efficiently without a budget, and your finances are really no different. The Personal Budget Planner included here will enable you not only to summarize where you earn and spend your money now but also to plan for the future. This is what budgeting is all about. You know where you can cut down on expenses, and it is up to you and you alone to do so.

> To spend is human; to save is divine.

As you project your future expenses, be sure to take into account the many bills you pay on a less than monthly basis. It is these whopping bills that get so many of us in trouble. As luck would have it, most of them seem to come due at the same time, so just when we think we've got our expenses under control, whammo, we owe our soul to some unfriendly insurance company. These are the kinds of expenses I'm talking about:

- Property taxes
- Homeowner's/renter's insurance
- Life insurance
- Other insurance
- Home improvements/maintenance
- Furniture
- Christmas/holidays
- Tuition
- Club membership dues
- Charitable contributions
- Estimated taxes
- IRA, Keogh, or other retirement plan contributions
- Vacation
- Seasonal fuel/electricity

If you never want to worry about these expenses again, add up how much they amount to annually, and each month deposit one-twelfth of that amount into a separate savings account. Of course, you must resist temptation and pay only those bills out of the account.

PERSONAL BUDGET PLANNER

Individuals and families should prepare budgets, as businesses do. This Personal Budget Planner can be used to record your past cash receipts and cash disbursements and/or to budget future receipts and disbursements. You may want to use the first column to record your past receipts and disbursements, the second column to list your budget over the next month, quarter, or year, and the third column to compare your actual future receipts and disbursements against your budget in the second column. If you budget over a period of less than one year, be sure to take into consideration those expenses that you pay less frequently than monthly, such as insurance, vacations, and tuition. You should be setting aside an amount each month that will eventually cover those large bills.

Indicate at the top of each column whether the amounts in that column are actual or estimated past figures or budgeted future figures. Also indicate the time period in each column—e.g., "July 1992" or "Year 1993."

Indicate if actual or budget: ....
Indicate the time period: ....

CASH RECEIPTS
  1. Gross salary $............... $............... $...............
  2. Interest ....
  3. Dividends ....
  4. Bonuses/profit sharing ....
  5. Alimony/child support
     received ....
  6. Distributions from
     partnerships ....
  7. Income from outside
     businesses ....
  8. Trust distributions ....
  9. Pension ....
10. Social Security ....
11. Gifts ....
12. Proceeds from sale of
     investments ....
13. Other
    ■............................... ....
    ■............................... ....
    ■............................... ....
14. Total cash receipts $............... $............... $...............

CASH DISBURSEMENTS
  1. Housing (rent/mortgage) $............... $............... $...............
  2. Food ....
  3. Household maintenance ....
  4. Utilities and telephone ....
  5. Clothing ....
  6. Personal care ....
  7. Medical and dental care ....
  8. Automobile/transportation ....
  9. Child care expenses ....
10. Entertainment ....
11. Vacation(s) ....

12. Gifts	....	....	....
13. Contributions	....	....	....
14. Insurance	....	....	....
15. Miscellaneous out-of-pocket expenses	....	....	....
16. Furniture	....	....	....
17. Home improvements	....	....	....
18. Real estate taxes	....	....	....
19. Loan payments	....	....	....
20. Credit card payments	....	....	....
21. Alimony/child support payments	....	....	....
22. Tuition/educational expenses	....	....	....
23. Business and professional expenses	....	....	....
24. Savings/investments	....	....	....
25. Income and Social Security taxes	....	....	....
26. Other			
■...............................	....	....	....
■...............................	....	....	....
■............................... $............	$............	$............	$............
27. Total cash disbursements	$............	$............	$............
Excess (Shortfall) of Cash Receipts over Cash Disbursements	$............	$............	$............

BETTER LIVING THROUGH ELECTRONICS

The easiest way to save money is never to see it. Bankers and credit union managers have told me time and again that the customers who really amass a lot of money over the years do it through payroll deduction or by some other means of having their money taken from them regularly—*electronically*! It doesn't have to be taken out of your paycheck. Most financial institutions (including mutual fund companies) are more than happy to help you not to see your money, and all you have to do is authorize them to withdraw a certain amount of money from your checking account each week or each month and place it in some investment account. But however you choose to save, be sure to save regularly. By the way, the next time you or your spouse's salary increases, increase the amount of savings that you have deducted from your paycheck or bank account. If you are fortunate enough to be able to take out a bonus or other distribution from your business, try to think about ways to save and invest at least a portion of it rather than spend it all. It's not really that painful.

GOOD DEBT, BAD DEBT

Interest on debt used to save higher-income people a lot on their taxes. But times have changed. Consumer indebtedness, which is just about all kinds of debt except home mortgages and investments loans, is no longer tax deductible. Even tax-deductible debt doesn't save much in taxes anymore since tax rates are now so much lower than they used to be. Interest amounting to $10,000 used to save a high-income taxpayer $5,000 in federal income taxes. It currently saves far less than that, if it is deductible at all. Any way you cut it, debt is less attractive than it used to be, but judging by the ever-increasing level of credit card indebtedness, that hasn't deterred many people from borrowing.

Debt can be very beneficial, or it can be detrimental. Just as you can distinguish between essential spending and frivolous spending, you know that there are good reasons to borrow and bad reasons to borrow. If you list your current loans and what they were used to purchase, you will be able to make that distinction easily.

THE KEYS TO GOOD DEBT MANAGEMENT

The best way to manage personal debt is to borrow only for appropriate reasons and to pay off the loans within a reasonable period of time. Good debt finances something worthwhile that will benefit you well into the future. Bad debt usually finances something you use up almost immediately or from which you never receive any real benefit (borrowing to consolidate loans, for example). Thus, a home mortgage is good debt, and credit card indebtedness is almost always bad debt. Borrowing to invest in real estate can be either good or bad, depending on how the

Say no to spending. Get high on saving.

investment fares. Unfortunately, some investors buy into real estate projects that are doomed from the outset.

All loans should be paid off as soon as possible—ideally, long before the asset you purchased with the loan stops benefiting you. Car loans are a special case, since they involve borrowing to buy a depreciating asset. Therefore, a car should be financed over no more than two to three years although the average car loan is now almost five years. If you borrow for much more than two years, you will be incurring repair bills while still making loan payments on your metal (and plastic) master. This is hardly an appealing situation. If you can't afford to finance a car over less than three years, you can't afford that car. Just because you own a business and can have a company car does not justify owning or leasing a car you cannot comfortably afford. Many small business owners end up saddling themselves with expensive cars and later regretting it since the money could be used elsewhere much more productively.

HOME SWEET HOME MORTGAGE

You may benefit handsomely by accelerating the repayment of your home mortgage. As a general rule of thumb, unless you can earn a return on an investment that is greater than the interest rate on your mortgage, you are better off making an additional payment against your mortgage. Don't spend every last dime trying to reduce your mortgage, however. You should always keep sufficient resources on hand to tide you and, if necessary, your business over in case of an emergency. Aside from that, however, accelerating the repayment of the mortgage can save a great deal of money.

> EXAMPLE: Ruth Ruggs, the owner of a carpet mill, recently took out a $100,000, 30-year, fixed mortgage at 10 percent interest. Her monthly mortgage payment is $878. If she pays another $197 per month against the mortgage, she will pay off the loan in 15 years, rather than 30 years, and save around $90,000 on the total after-tax cost of the mortgage.

You should try, if possible, to pay off your mortgage by the time you retire, because it will greatly reduce the amount of income you will need to retire comfortably.

Mortgage refinancing is another matter you may want to address if you currently have a high-interest fixed-rate mortgage or if you are uncomfortable with your adjustable-rate mortgage. While some rules of thumb may help you assess whether the time is right to consider refinancing, you will have to put pencil to paper to decide. You must weigh the costs of refinancing against the longer-term interest savings. But if you expect to stay in the house for the next several years and prevailing interest rates are 1 or 2 percent lower than your current mortgage rate, you may benefit from refinancing, particularly if current fixed mortgage rates are in the single digits.

HELs BELLS

Hardly a day goes by without some lender ringing the bells in celebration of home equity loans—and with good reason. HELs are one of the best loan arrangements ever invented—for the lenders, anyway. What they're pushing is a variable rate secured loan. A lender can't ask for much more than that. What you're getting is a convenient, and perhaps tempting, source of money, the interest on which, depending on your circumstances, is probably tax deductible. For good managers of family credit, home equity loans may be the preferable borrowing source. For the easily tempted they can be downright dangerous.

To be useful, home equity credit lines must be managed like any other loan—by paying off the outstanding balance over an appropriate period of time. If you draw on your credit line to pay income taxes or to take a vacation (either of which should have been anticipated and otherwise provided for), the loan balance should be paid off quickly—within a few months at most. If you use the credit line to buy a car, pay it off over two or three years, just as you should an automobile loan. There are only a couple of uses of home equity loan money, or any loan money for that matter, that would justify a long repayment period. First is if you make *substantive* improvements to your home in lieu of moving. Substantive does not mean a swimming pool or bocce court but something that adds significant value to your home, like adding another bedroom or remodeling your kitchen. A long repayment term may also be justified if you use the money to pay college tuition for your children. If you do hock the home for this very worthwhile purpose, you should do so only after all other possible scholarship, grant, and loan sources have been exhausted.

If you are about to withdraw some money from your business, remember that there is no law saying you are required to spend it. It is perfectly legal to save it.

There may come a time when you will have to decide whether to use a home equity loan to provide needed resources for your business. This is a very difficult decision, of course, because you may be jeopardizing your home if the business cannot generate sufficient income to repay the loan. Therefore, any such use of home equity credit, or any other type of personal loan for that matter, must be made only after a thorough and realistic evaluation. You may well want to solicit the advice of your accountant, lawyer, or another trusted and objective third party.

PLANNING TO MEET LIFE'S MAJOR EXPENSES

BUYING A FIRST HOME

One of the best things you can do to achieve financial independence is to buy a home, whether it's a house, condominium, cooperative, duplex, triplex, or town house. For most people, the advantages of owning far outweigh the disadvantages. True, interest rates may be high and housing prices flat or declining. Some people wait around for ideal conditions—low interest rates and housing prices that are low but poised to go through the stratosphere. These people usually become permanent renters because conditions will never be so ideal. Don't worry too much about current conditions. Concentrate instead on saving for the down payment, becoming familiar with the local real estate market, and putting your overall finances in good order so you can qualify for a mortgage. Lenders are getting stricter, so don't be surprised if they make you jump through hoops before granting the mortgage. Since you are self-employed, you will probably encounter even more difficulty in obtaining a mortgage because of the uncertainty of your future income. But if you are diligent and have been disciplined in your personal and business financial planning, you will get the mortgage. Finally, don't set your sights too high on a first home. Most first-time homebuyers start out in a home and neighborhood that aren't quite as nice as the ones they grew up in. Eventually you'll be able to trade up, but for

---

There has to be divine guidance in life because spenders tend to marry savers.

now the important thing is to get into that first home. You'll probably be temporarily impoverished by the home purchase, but that's good practice for future "life events" that may also impoverish you, such as educating the kids.

EDUCATING YOUR CHILDREN

Have you educated yourself on education costs? Educating the children is, for many parents, one of their biggest financial challenges. Careful planning is essential. The only thing that can be said for certain about future college costs is that they will continue to outpace inflation. You should probably assume that your children will not qualify for any financial aid. For example, right now a family with total assets of $80,000 including the equity in their home and with total income of $60,000 would probably *not* qualify for any financial aid for a child in college. Even if you enjoy a comfortable income, you may still have difficulty meeting college tuition bills. Fortunately, colleges and lending institutions have invented innovative ways to help beleaguered families meet these costs. Many colleges offer tuition prepayment plans that allow you to pay for all four years of college at the first year's rate. Some colleges even lend parents the funds to do this with extended repayment schedules of up to fifteen years. The College Education Funding Forecaster included can help you project how much you will need to save to meet college education costs.

Loan sources are more abundant than outright assistance, but overreliance on loans can end up saddling you or your child with too much debt. If you take the time to evaluate loan sources carefully, you will often be rewarded by uncovering loans with lower interest rates and more flexible repayment schedules.

And one last thing. Don't rely on what your friends say about college financial aid matters. Conditions change so rapidly that the tips they give are probably out-of-date. Good information is available from local high schools and colleges as well as from numerous publications.

EXPANDING YOUR BUSINESS

If you are contemplating expanding your existing business or starting another business, you probably need not be forewarned about the risks. Some business owners and self-employed professionals, intoxicated by their initial success,

COLLEGE EDUCATION FUNDING FORECASTER WORK SHEET

This form can be used to estimate how much you will need to save each year in order to fund future college expenses. The College Education Cost Forecaster projects average college education costs for a four-year public or private school education. The College Education Savings Estimator calculates how much you will have to save to meet those costs.

College Education Cost Forecaster

The following table projects current average four-year education costs compiled by the College Board, assuming a 6% annual increase in costs. These figures can be used as a guide in estimating the costs of college for your child or children.

Year Entering	Public School	Private School	Selective Private School
1991	$24,405	$ 62,104	$ 87,690
1992	25,870	65,831	92,951
1993	27,422	69,780	98,528
1994	29,067	73,967	104,440
1995	30,811	78,405	110,706
1996	32,660	83,110	117,348
1997	34,620	88,096	124,389
1998	36,697	93,382	131,853
1999	38,899	98,985	139,764
2000	41,232	104,923	148,150
2001	43,706	111,219	157,039
2002	46,329	117,893	166,461
2003	49,109	124,966	176,449
2004	52,055	132,464	187,036
2005	55,178	140,412	198,258
2006	58,489	148,837	210,153
2007	61,998	157,767	222,762
2008	65,718	167,233	236,127
2009	69,661	177,267	250,295
2010	73,841	187,903	265,313

College Education Savings Estimator

Name of Child _____ _____ _____ Total

1. Total estimated
   college costs
   (from above) $............. $............. $............. $.............

2. Amount of
   savings
   currently
   available for
   college (A) $............. $............. $.............

3. Multiplied by
   appreciation
   factor (from
   table below)(B) x............. x............. x.............

4. Equals
   estimated
   amount of
   current savings
   available at
   college age (line
   2 times line 3) $............. $............. $.............

5. Estimated
   amount of costs
   remaining to be
   funded (line 1
   minus line 4) $............. $............. $.............

6. Adjustments(C) $............. $............. $............. $.............

7. Equals amount
   that you wish to
   accumulate by
   college age (line
   5 plus/minus
   line 6) $............. $............. $............. $.............

8. Multiplied by
   accumulation
   factor from table
   below (D) x............. x............. x.............

9. Equals the
   amount to be
   saved each year
   to meet future
   college costs (E) $............. $............. $............. $.............

APPRECIATION FACTOR TABLE FOR LINE 3				ACCUMULATION FACTOR TABLE FOR LINE 8			
Year Child Enters College	Factor	Year Child Enters College	Factor	Year Child Enters College	Factor	Year Child Enters College	Factor
1991	1.07	2001	2.11	1991	.483	2001	.056
1992	1.15	2002	2.25	1992	.311	2002	.050
1993	1.23	2003	2.41	1993	.225	2003	.044
1994	1.31	2004	2.58	1994	.174	2004	.040
1995	1.40	2005	2.76	1995	.140	2005	.036
1996	1.50	2006	2.94	1996	.116	2006	.032
1997	1.60	2007	3.15	1997	.097	2007	.027
1998	1.72	2008	3.37	1998	.083	2008	.027
1999	1.84	2009	3.61	1999	.072	2009	.024
2000	1.97	2010	3.87	2000	.063	2010	.022

A. Indicate on Line 2 any savings you now have that are earmarked to pay education costs. Many parents with more than one child simply divide these savings equally among the children, unless the savings or investment accounts are in a specified child's name.

B. The appreciation factor on Line 3 is provided in the above table. It recognizes the future increase in value of the savings or investments that you presently have earmarked for college costs. The factor assumes a 7% annual increase in value.

C. Many parents will want to make adjustments in Line 6 to the estimated amount of college costs to be funded. Reductions might be appropriate in situations where financial aid can reasonably be anticipated or where the child will be expected to contribute to college costs through summer or school-year income. Additions to the estimated costs to be funded will be appropriate if, for example, parents expect the child to go to a college that is more expensive than average. Selective private colleges, in particular, may be considerably more expensive than the averages provided on this work sheet.

D. The accumulation factor to be entered on Line 8 is provided in the above table. Multiplying this factor by the amount of money you wish to accumulate by college age will show the amount of money you would need to save each year to accumulate the necessary funds. An annual return of 7% is assumed.

E. Parents are often dismayed by the amount of money they would have to save each year to meet future college costs (Line 9). Don't be discouraged, however. The important thing is to begin a regular savings program even if it's only a portion of the amount indicated. Remember also that the annual amount to be saved assumes *level* payment. Even if you can afford to save only a portion of the amount indicated on Line 9, you will still be able to accumulate a nest egg that will go a long way toward easing the financial burden of your children's education. It is often more realistic for parents gradually to increase the amount of money they set aside each year.

decide to expand or get into new businesses that end up draining the resources generated by the successful business. Even the largest corporations sometimes stumble by doing the same thing. Therefore, you should be particularly careful to plan any such course of action far in advance, in consultation with a lawyer or accountant experienced in advising people in similar businesses.

They will be able to help you with a number of important matters in addition to recommending whether or not you should proceed, including the best way to organize the business; if you are acquiring an existing business, they can advise you as to an appropriate price to pay for it.

Unless you are awash with cash, you will also have to finance the expansion or acquisition. You must not, however, saddle your business or yourself with too much debt. You will have to prepare projections of estimated revenues and expenses from the incremental business just as you hopefully budget for your existing business. Don't let the excitement of building an empire cloud your good judgment. But if you plan carefully, and retain and use experienced counsel, you will be well on your way to financial independence.

Below is a Spending and Borrowing Action Plan to help you keep your expenses under control. Now that you have a clear picture of your current financial situation and a solid foundation to work from, it's time to move on to that appealing and elusive stage, accumulating wealth.

SPENDING AND BORROWING ACTION PLAN

CURRENT STATUS

Needs Action	Okay or Not Applicable	
☐	☐	1. Save at least 10 percent of your gross income.
☐	☐	2. Maintain a life-style that your current and expected future income can support comfortably.
☐	☐	3. If you are enjoying unusually high income as a result of your business endeavors, don't increase your spending; rather, increase your saving.
☐	☐	4. Prepare a budget from time to time to summarize your personal income and expenditures.
☐	☐	5. If you have trouble paying large bills, set up a separate savings account for that purpose.

Needs Action	*Okay or Not Applicable*	
☐	☐	6. Create an "emergency" savings fund equal to at least three months personal expenses or more if you may eventually have to use personal resources to support yourself and/or your business in the event of a business downturn.
☐	☐	7. Borrow only for worthwhile purposes. Be particularly careful in using personally borrowed money to support your business.
☐	☐	8. If you can afford it, make additional payments on your home mortgage from time to time.
☐	☐	9. If and when conditions warrant, consider refinancing your home in the current interest rate environment.
☐	☐	10. If applicable, take action now to provide for your children's education.
☐	☐	11. If you are contemplating expanding your business or acquiring another business, weigh the risks carefully, and consult with experienced professional advisers.

Comments: . . . .
. . . .
. . . .
. . . .
. . . .
. . . .

Spending and Borrowing "To Do" List:. . . . .
. . . .
. . . .
. . . .
. . . .
. . . .

II

ACCUMULATING WEALTH

4 | Profiting from Wise Investing

Investing wisely is arguably the most important thing you will do to achieve financial security. It's just about as easy to make good investments as it is to make dumb investments. Most people don't make dumb investments on their own; rather, someone encourages them. Therefore, this chapter and Chapter 5 will help you become a better investor—one who can make sensible investment decisions independent of a biased outsider's suggestions. These chapters emphasize investing in each of three major categories—stock investments, interest-earning investments, and real estate investments. Nevertheless, you should not lose sight of other important "investments" that, directly or indirectly, will contribute to your ultimate financial success, including your own business, your pension plans, your home, good health, and a stable personal life.

As the following diagram illustrates, investing is really the focal point of the personal financial planning process.

As important as investing is, most people don't do a very good job at it. What's the secret to successful investing? First you must decide what you want to accomplish with your investments. Generally, you will ultimately want to use them to provide retirement income, although you may be interrupted along the

Investing Is the Focal Point of the Personal Financial Planning Process

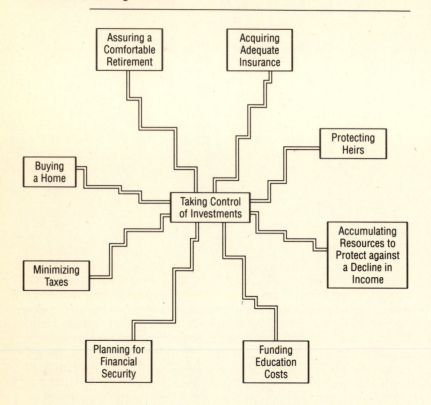

way to meet such important needs as buying a first home and educating the children. As corny as it sounds, if you don't have some clearly identified idea of what you're going to do with the money, you're not going to be able to organize your investments to meet those targets. Once you have set realistic objectives, you can then go about making investments that will help you achieve them. The right kinds of investments are undoubtedly ones you are already pretty familiar with. They are not new types of investments, nor are they the kinds of investments you have to buy and sell all the time. In a word, they're *old-fashioned*. Finally, successful investors, whether they invest themselves or use investment advisers, won't let anyone persuade them to alter their objectives or their investments significantly.

EXAMPLE: A good friend of mine who is a very successful stockbroker as well as radio talk show host related the following true story to me: "A few years ago a recently retired man came into my office to ask for some investment advice. He said that he was very embarrassed about his situation and had avoided speaking with an investment adviser about it for several years. About twenty-five years earlier he had inherited $40,000 worth of stock from his father. He told me that at that time he didn't know anything about investments, although he recognized the names of all the companies whose shares he had inherited. So he put the stock certificates in his safe-deposit box, where they sat for twenty-five years. He then went on to say that he had been receiving dividend income all along, and he noted that it had increased considerably over the years. I told him to retrieve the certificates from the safe-deposit box so we could figure out what they were worth. Well, as you might suspect, his stock was now worth over $500,000. I shudder to think what would have happened if he had asked someone to manage these investments actively over the past twenty-five years rather than having put them in the safe-deposit box." The moral of this story: Sometimes the best thing to do with your investments is nothing.

Many self-employed professionals and small business owners have particular difficulty investing appropriately and sufficiently since their businesses often consume all of their time and most of their resources. Ultimately, however, most independent businesspeople will need to accumulate resources outside of their business if they are going to achieve financial security. Among the issues that make investment planning for self-employed people unique are:

■ Many self-employed professionals and small business owners either do not offer a pension plan in their business, or the plan that is in place will not, in and of itself, provide sufficient resources to assure a comfortable retirement. Depending on your circumstances, you will have to accumulate considerably more personal investments in order to achieve financial security by retirement age than if you worked for a company with larger retirement benefits.

■ Independent businesspeople must always be prepared for periods of lower income due to a downturn in their business. This means, among other things, that the need for a substantial "emergency fund" as well as the ability to turn this money into cash quickly may be particularly important. Successful independent businesspeople often fail to manage their investments appropriately. They are often too busy running their businesses to devote sufficient time to learn about their investments and manage them efficiently. They may rely too heavily on investment advisers as a result. Also, some independent businesspeople take too much risk in their personal investments, not realizing that the risk inherent in their own small business means their investments outside of the business should be invested more conservatively.

■ Many self-employed professionals and small business owners fail to exploit their own unique abilities to identify and invest in areas where they have a particular advantage. For example, owners of small manufacturing companies may be aware of promising publicly held companies through discussions or dealings with their vendors or customers.

In this chapter you will learn how to set reasonable investment objectives so you *can* learn to be a better investor. In the next chapter you will learn how to manage your investments better, whether you are actively managing them yourself or relying on others to advise you.

SETTING OBJECTIVES

Everyone's primary financial planning goal is financial security—which means that your investments (combined with Social Security and pension benefits) will provide you and your dependents with an adequate income for the rest of your life. In essence, financial security means you can afford to retire. Some people achieve financial security sooner than others. Some people never achieve it. Most of us want to be financially secure no later than retirement age.

It is very difficult for most self-employed professionals and small business owners to build up their businesses to the point where they can be sold for a great deal of money. The goodwill created by successful businesses does not necessarily command a significant price from the eventual buyer of the business. Therefore, you must be particularly careful to assure that you set aside enough money on a regular basis to provide for any unforeseen business or personal contingencies as well as an adequate retirement.

Accumulating sufficient personal investments is the single most important component of financial security. As an independent businessperson, you have three major categories of investments. The first is your business, which at a minimum provides you with the opportunity to generate sufficient income to accumulate personal investment capital. The business *may* also be able to be sold in the future, thereby creating additional personal wealth. The second investment area is personal savings and investments that are accumulated outside the business. The third investment area involves money that you have set aside in retirement plans. The contents of this chapter apply to both your personal investments and your retirement investments. You need to make a judgment as to whether or not your business interests will be able to command additional investment money in the future. I caution you, however, to be realistic since many an entrepreneur has been sorely disappointed upon finding out that the business he or she has worked so hard to build up over the years cannot be sold for an amount sufficient to assure financial security. Also, remember that financial security requires that all areas of financial planning, including insurance, tax planning, and estate planning, be attended to. For example, you may eventually accumulate a lot of money, but if you are not properly and completely insured, you are not financially secure. (Such topics are discussed throughout this book.)

One of the most important elements of long-term investment success is *consistency*. Too many people throw their money away blindly following "hot" market tips and their (commissioned) purveyor's breathless recommendations of financial products with seductive sales raps but dubious merit—for example, "unbundled stock units," "payment-in-kind preferred stock," or "equity index participations." Whether you are just embarking on a saving and investing program or are in midvoyage, you need to establish and periodically review your investment objectives. Objectives need to be clearly articulated in each of the following areas:

1. The amount of percentage of earnings to be set aside periodically for investment purposes. If you aren't yet sure how much you will need to save, you can get a better idea in Chapter 6, where you will figure out how much you need to save to be able to retire comfortably.

2. A reasonable target long-term rate of return on investments. Permit me to give you a target. You should strive to earn a return on your investments that exceeds inflation by at least 3 percent after taxes. This is easier said than done, however. I would suggest that for planning purposes you assume a 4 percent to 5 percent long-term inflation rate. As the example below indicates, if your combined federal and state personal income tax rate is 33 percent, you would have to earn a 12 percent return on a taxable interest-earning investment such as a CD in order to beat inflation by 3 percent after taxes. It'll be less confusing after the example.

EXAMPLE:

Comparison of Interest-Earning Investments That Pay 10% Interest and 12% Interest.

	Rate of Return	
	10%	12%
Pretax income on a $10,000 investment	$1,000	$1,200
Federal income tax (28%)	(280)	(336)
State income tax (5%)	(50)	(60)
Total tax	(330)	(396)
After-tax income	$ 670	$ 804
After-tax return on the $10,000 investment	6.7%	8.0%

If the inflation rate is 5 percent, the investment that pays 10 percent interest beats inflation by only 1.7 percent, whereas the 12 percent return investment (if one can be found) beats inflation by 3 percent.

Most investors don't realize the impact of taxes. When CD rates reach 9 or 10 percent, many investors think they have died and gone to heaven. Yet, on an after-tax basis, they are staying just ahead of inflation. On the other hand, these rates are *very* attractive for retirement-oriented accounts since retirement funds are not taxed until they are withdrawn at retirement. So an 8.5 percent CD is growing at 8.5 percent per year—well ahead of inflation. This is one of many good reasons why you need to maximize your retirement account contributions and take advantage of other sensible tax-deferred investments discussed in Chapter 7. Small business owners and self-employed professionals, in particular, should take advantage of the retirement plan tax breaks available to them.

3. The third objective involves the allocation of your investments among the three major investment categories, which are stocks, interest-earning securities, and real estate, so that you will be able to achieve the desired rate of return without subjecting your investments to undue risk. These matters are discussed in Chapter 5.

MAXIMIZING YOUR INVESTMENT SAVVY WITH A MINIMUM TIME INVESTMENT

Before you can take control of your own finances, you must have at least some understanding of the various types of investments available. The more understanding you gain, the better, but the demands of running a business may prevent you from becoming an investment expert or staying up-to-date with the ever-changing investment markets. However, those who have too little knowledge of or interest in investments are more often than not going to suffer, either at the hands of opportunistic "advisers" or by just plain overlooking or avoiding an appropriate investment.

EXAMPLE: A couple who owned several automobile dealerships recently asked me to review their personal financial situation. This couple had worked very hard in building up a rather successful business. Over the past ten years they had managed to withdraw more from the business than they needed to meet living expenses. Unfortunately, they did not invest this money as well as they could have. Over the years their personal and retirement plan money had been invested exclusively in bank savings accounts, money market funds, and short-term tax-exempt securities. While the owners were correct in saying that because of the risks inherent in the automobile dealership business they wanted their "outside money" invested safely, there is such a thing as being too conservative in investing. A more appropriate portfolio would have consisted of at least some stock investments and some longer-term interest-earning investments.

I have also seen entrepreneurs who have taken too much risk rather than too little with their personal resources. Many successful businesspeople fancy themselves as experts in assessing risk and, therefore, end up putting their money in all manner of high-risk speculative stock and real estate ventures. As you will see, the key to successful investing is to avoid investing in extremes and to maintain a well-balanced portfolio that is appropriate to your particular circumstances.

The following table will help you understand the kinds of commonly used and usually sensible investments that you might include in your portfolio. Some may be suitable for you, others not. It depends on your objectives. The table is organized according to the three major investment categories: stock, interest-earning, and real estate. Within each category, the investment securities are organized according to the way in which you purchase and own them, whether directly by buying the securities yourself, indirectly through mutual funds, or in the case of real estate, through limited partnerships. The fine points of investing are discussed in Chapter 5.

Investment Bill of Fare

COMMON STOCK INVESTMENTS

Directly owned (owning shares of stock of individual companies):

Income stocks pay a high dividend and are usually in fairly stable industries, like public utilities. Popular with retirees and bank trust departments.

Growth stocks are bought for capital appreciation, because they pay little or no dividend. They can be as volatile as all get out.

Blue chip stocks are sometimes referred to as "Blue Gyp" stocks. High-quality, steadily increasing dividend. A lot of wealthy families got that way by investing solely in blue chips, which should tell you something.

Cyclical stocks are shares of companies whose earnings tend to fluctuate with their business cycles, such as steel and housing. Cyclicals don't always behave like the pundits say they should; otherwise, no one would own his or her shares when the business cycle turns down.

Speculative stocks are brilliant investments if they go up. Otherwise it's gambling, but certainly a better form of gambling than playing the lottery, which is nothing more than a tax on the naive. As with any form of gambling, don't bet heavily on speculative issues.

Indirectly owned (owning shares of mutual funds, which invest in stock of many corporations):

Aggressive growth funds, also known as maximum capital gains funds, seek the greatest possible gain, and often invest in speculative stocks. They do great in bull markets and terribly in bear markets. Long-term holders of these funds have been amply rewarded in the past.

Growth and income funds aim for a reasonable return by combining growth stocks with higher quality dividend-paying stocks. More conservative than aggressive growth funds, and still turn in solid returns.

Balanced funds usually invest about half their assets or more in stocks and the balance in bonds or other debt instruments. Good way to get an instantly diversified stock-and-bond portfolio, for an investment of $1,000 or less. My favorite investment.

International funds are the only efficient way to invest in foreign stocks, and foreign stocks belong in every well-diversified portfolio.

Gold funds invest in, you guessed it, gold, or more likely, the shares of gold-mining companies. People hold gold as a hedge against inflation. Short of buying and storing the bullion (ingots make very impressive paperweights), this is the best way to play the gold market.

INTEREST-EARNING INVESTMENTS

Directly owned (owning the securities of individual bond or certificate issuers):

Treasury securities are the means by which the U.S. government borrows money and as you know, they're pretty good at borrowing money. Treasury bills, notes, and bonds are issued regularly by the Federal government and are a popular investment, particularly for people who are averse to risk and to paying state income taxes.

Mortgage-backed securities have names that sound like characters on *Hee Haw,* like Ginnie Mae, Fannie Mae, and Freddie Mac. These investments represent interests in pools of mortgages. Their relatively high yields have been attracting a lot of investor interest, but their high investment minimums, typically $25,000, keep out the riffraff.

Municipal bonds don't appeal to people who enjoy paying federal income taxes, which means they're very popular. If you purchase bonds of issuing authorities in your own state (or bonds of Puerto Rico), you escape state income taxes and, perhaps, local income taxes.

Corporate bonds, of course, represent debt obligations of corporations and vary significantly in quality, from triple-A rated all the way down to junk bonds. Purchasers of junk bonds (issuers prefer to call them "high yield" bonds) know well the perils of blindly chasing the highest yielding corporate bond issues.

Certificates of deposit are interest-bearing deposits with banks, with a specified maturity that typically ranges from thirty days to five or more years. Federally insured CDs are a major form of investment for many people. They shouldn't be, because better yields are usually available through other interest-earning investments.

Indirectly owned (owning shares of fixed-income mutual funds or money market funds, which, in turn, own interest-earning debt obligations of many issuers):

Government securities funds invest in Treasury securities and/or mortgage-backed securities. Low investment minimums on these funds provide investors of all means with access to the government securities markets.

Municipal bond funds are available, including single-state funds that provide double tax exemption to residents of a particular state. Similar to all mutual funds that invest in long-term debt obligations, muni funds can decline in value if prevailing interest rates rise.

Corporate bond funds pay higher interest than municipal funds, but what you have left over after paying income taxes on the interest paid out by the corporate bond fund is what matters. Similar to municipal bond funds, each corporate bond fund states in its prospectus the quality of the bonds it will buy for its portfolio. Therefore, investors can select funds that invest in anywhere from the highest to the lowest quality bonds.

Money market funds invest in short-term, usually very safe and stable securities including commercial paper (short-term IOUs of large U.S. corporations), Treasury bills, and large bank CDs. Money funds are a very convenient place to stash your money and allow it to earn at least some interest while stashed.

REAL ESTATE INVESTMENTS

Directly owned (owning and managing a real estate investment):
Income-producing real estate can range from a rented condominium unit to an apartment building to commercial properties. Attractive investments with possible tax benefits, although many independent businesspeople lack the time or inclination to manage income-producing real estate.
Undeveloped land ties up a lot of money for a long time. Land in particularly desirable areas is very expensive, but, with some luck, it will appreciate smartly.

Indirectly owned (purchasing an interest in a real estate limited partnership):
Real estate limited partnerships, once the darling of tax shelter devotees, have fallen on hard times. The loss of tax benefits, combined with overbuilding in many locales, has left many limited partnership investors disillusioned—and a lot poorer. Attractive deals are still possible, but buyer beware!

Once you become familiar with the different types of investments, you need to understand the concept of a "balanced portfolio" and decide how best to allocate your own resources among the three major categories of investment assets: stock investments, interest-earning investments, and real estate investments. Don't confuse this with the notion of "market timing" that is currently in vogue. Market timing means that someone purports to be able to divine the optimum proportion of assets that should be invested in the various investment categories at any point in time. Of course, these proportions change faster than Bolivia's government. Short-term market timing just doesn't work well. On the other hand, the concept of asset allocation is terribly important in planning your "permanent portfolio structure." In short, you need to establish some general parameters to guide your portfolio mix, for example, "My portfolio will consist roughly of 40 percent stocks, 30 percent bonds, and 30 percent real estate." More on this is in the next chapter.

When you understand the many good investments that are available and their appropriate proportions in your portfolio, you can manage your investments more effectively. By familiarizing yourself with market conditions periodically and by applying some straightforward rules of thumb, you will be able to improve the performance of your investments. Believe me, it is not very difficult to be a good investor.

SOME GENERAL INVESTMENT RULES OF THUMB

Invest with a long-term view. Although your broker may not want me to say this, the buy-and-hold strategy of investing usually produces much better results (for the investor) than an actively traded portfolio. Studies have shown that over most holding periods of ten years or longer, investors in stocks have enjoyed returns well in excess of inflation; shorter holding periods generally produce much lower returns. Also, if you take a long-term perspective, you will certainly fret less over shorter-term market vacillations.

Buy quality. Quality investments offer a good measure of protection, particularly in times of market volatility and investment uncertainty. Stocks and bonds of well-established companies and/or well-located real estate investments have greater staying power when market conditions deteriorate. Buy only those mutual funds that have produced above-average performance over the past five to ten years.

Don't borrow to invest in anything except real estate. The investors who were really hurt by the adverse bond and stock market conditions of 1987 were generally those who borrowed "on margin" to increase their investments. The only way for them to cover their margin calls was to sell their holdings at an inopportune time. While borrowing for real estate can be an effective means of increasing investment returns, heavily margined stock and bond investors expose themselves to considerable risk.

Avoid high-risk investments. While you may think they offer you a one-way ticket to nirvana, commodities, futures, coins, and buying stock options are, for the most part, suckers' games. If you want to make high-risk investments, feel free so long as you use

---

The only three reasons why your stockbroker would want you to sell a stock:
1. It has fallen in value and doesn't look as good as it once did. There are better opportunities in other stocks.
2. It's at the same price as when you bought it; it just isn't moving. There are better opportunities in other stocks.
3. It has risen in value. Let's lock in your profits now. There are better opportunities in other stocks. (This occurrence is exceedingly rare but has been known to happen.)

Ten percent "sure" is better than 25 percent "maybe."

---

only a small portion of your portfolio. Just be prepared to lose the money because, more often than not, lose it you will.

Avoid new investments. Don't buy anything new like a new stock issue (you probably aren't important enough to your broker to be offered an issue that will rise in value), a new closed-end fund (they almost always go down in value), a new piece of real estate (it doesn't have a rent history), or a new and improved type of security. Don't be a guinea pig.

Shop around for the best interest rates on interest-earning investments. Take advantage of competition in the marketplace by shopping for the best rates. For example, ask your broker to quote a "brokered CD" rate. CDs that are sold through brokers often pay higher interest than you can fetch at your local bank. The same goes for money market funds. Money market mutual funds usually offer much higher yields than bank money market deposit accounts.

Vary the maturities on interest-earning investments. You should avoid concentrating the maturities of your interest-earning investments. For example, rather than buy a single two-year CD, consider splitting it up among a one-year, a two-year, and a five-year CD. By "staggering" (also known as "laddering") maturities, you will avoid being stuck with, say, a lot of long-term bonds during a period of rising interest rates. If you were, the value of your bonds would drop, and therefore you are truly "stuck" with low-interest-rate investments. Another thing you can do with interest-earning investments is to time their maturities to coincide with years when you will need the cash: for example, when the children are in college or during your retirement years. If you invest in bond mutual funds, you can still stagger maturities by dividing your fund investments up among short-term, intermediate-term, and longer-term bond funds.

If someone who is trying to sell you an investment can't explain it to your satisfaction in one sentence, don't buy it.

Buy no-load mutual funds. You will do yourself a favor by spending a little time researching mutual funds and selecting no-load mutual funds with low annual expenses. Rest assured that if you buy a fund through a broker, even if it's a "no load," the broker is getting paid, and it's coming out of your investment. Whatever your particular investment need, there's a true no-load fund that will meet it. Some fund families, including Dreyfus, Fidelity, T. Rowe Price, Twentieth Century, and Vanguard provide a multitude of excellent no-load or low-load funds that are operated very efficiently.

Investing is the focal point of successful personal financial planning. Yet many independent businesspeople don't do a very good job with their personal investments. Up to this point, we have laid the groundwork for a more detailed review of how you can "build" an investment portfolio that will help you on your way to achieving financial security. This is the subject of Chapter 5. But first you should review Table 4, which summarizes my personal and admittedly biased assessment of the suitability of various types of investments.

T A B L E 4

Pond's Assessment of Investment Suitability

TYPE OF INVESTMENT	ASSESSMENT
Equity Investments:	
Common stock	Has been, is, and will continue to be good long-term inflation hedge. Buy and hold.
Preferred stock	Not very exciting unless you want the dividend income.
Stock mutual funds	Good way to get diversification; cheap way to have your funds managed.
Options	For suckers or professional investors. You are probably not the latter and hopefully not the former.
Commodity futures	For the gullible.
Stock-index futures	Have a role in sophisticated portfolio

TYPE OF INVESTMENT	ASSESSMENT
	hedging strategies, which means they're not for you.
New issues	You don't pay commissions on new issues, which helps offset the loss most of them experience after you buy them.
Foreign stocks	There is always a bull market somewhere in the world. Difficult to evaluate, so use international mutual funds.
Precious metals	The only reason you should own a lot of gold is if you use it to fill teeth. Otherwise, no more than 5 to 10 percent of portfolio.
Collectibles	Nice to sit on, walk on, or look at. Don't expect to retire on the profits.

Interest-Earning Investments:

Certificates of deposit	Generally lackluster returns after you finish giving Uncle Sam his piece of the interest. Chances are your local bank doesn't offer the best rates you can get, so shop around.
Treasury securities	Yields fluctuate and usually become attractive once or twice per year. Safe, but how much safety do you need?
Mortgage-backed securities	Nice yields but ever-present danger of getting back principal as interest rates drop.
Municipal bonds	Compare muni returns against after-tax returns on taxable securities. You may well find munis to be preferable.
Corporate bonds	Okay if you can get a much better yield than Treasuries. Otherwise, they don't justify the risk.
Junk bonds	Reserved for people who like high income and deteriorating principal.
Foreign fixed-income investments	Emerging investment area that is highly specialized and usually subjects you to currency risk. Buy through mutual funds only.

TYPE OF INVESTMENT	ASSESSMENT
Fixed-income mutual funds	Good way to let someone else worry about the direction of interest rates. Offers diversification and inexpensive management.
Savings accounts	Better than nothing, but not much better. Keep emergency funds there only.
U.S. savings bonds	Nice gift; better than they used to be.
Money market funds	A temporary parking place only, please, since you can't beat inflation by very much on an after-tax basis. Money market mutual funds almost always beat bank money market accounts hands down.
Real Estate Investments:	
Income-producing real estate	The average person's best route to wealth, if you buy at the right price and can stomach being a landlord.
Undeveloped land	An expensive little lot is better than a lot of cheap lots. In other words, 50 square feet in Manhattan, New York, is a better investment than 50 square miles in Manhattan, Montana.
Limited partnerships	Probably a good investment—next century. In the meantime, perhaps one deal in a hundred is worthwhile.
Any "new" investment that comes along, like "Unbundled Stock Units"	Excellent money-making opportunity, *if* you happen to be selling them to an unsuspecting public.

INVESTMENT ACTION PLAN

CURRENT STATUS

*Needs   Okay or
Action   Not Applicable*

☐   ☐   1. Establish realistic investment objectives and review/revise them periodically.

☐   ☐   2. Make sure your investment objectives and planning recognize the economic expectations for your business.

☐   ☐   3. Become familiar with the variety of commonly used investment securities and assess how each might be used in your investment portfolio.

☐   ☐   4. Take advantage of any expertise you may have through your job experience that you may be able to apply to your investing.

☐   ☐   5. List below the three worst shortcomings you have that hinder or have hindered your investment success. The purpose of writing these down is to impress upon you that they should not be repeated.

1. . . . .
2. . . . .
3. . . . .

5 | Taking Inventory of Your Investments

Now that you've set reasonable investment goals and have a basic idea of the various kinds of investments and the issues involved in investing, you're ready to learn how to choose the best investments for you and how to evaluate and control your portfolio, no matter how small (or large) it might be. Don't be dismayed if you can count the total dollars of the personal investments you now have on the fingers of one hand, so long as you realize the importance of beginning sooner, rather than later, to save the money outside of your business that will allow you to accumulate sufficient resources to assure your financial security.

FOUR STEPS TO INVESTMENT SUCCESS

Since investing effectively is so important to your ultimate financial well-being, you need to develop a plan that will help guide you both in deciding on the types of investments to make and in reviewing your investments periodically. "Periodically" doesn't mean every day; otherwise, you'll become so concerned that you're likely to make investment changes too frequently. Rather, if you establish some sensible criteria now, you will be able to invest wisely and well without needing to spend an inordinate amount of time worrying about your investments. The four steps to investment success are:

Step One: Deciding how much of your portfolio should be invested in stock, interest-earning investments, and, perhaps, real estate.

Step Two: Once you have decided how much of your investments should be in a given investment category, you next need to determine whether you should purchase the securities directly by buying individual stock and interest-earning securities or indirectly via mutual funds and limited partnerships.

Step Three: Next, you need to determine within each category what classifications of investments might be appropriate— for example, for indirectly owned stocks, whether you should invest in aggressive growth stock mutual funds and/or international mutual funds.

Step Four: Finally, you need to select carefully specific investments within each category.

As you review the investment process, I will periodically refer to the "Investment Allocation" diagram that follows. It serves as the basis for your own investment decision making. If you aren't quite sure what kinds of investments fit in each of the boxes, they are listed and described in the "Investment Bill of Fare" that appears in Chapter 4. The following example shows how an appropriate investment "portfolio" can be put together.

Investment Allocation

Method of Ownership	Investment Category		
	Stock	Interest-Earning	Real Estate
Direct Ownership			
Indirect Ownership (Mutual Fund/ Partnership)			

EXAMPLE: Griese Spooner, the proprietor of a popular fast-food restaurant, has managed to set aside $25,000 dollars over the past few years, which is now sitting in a money market account. He has just read the above "Four Steps to Investment Success" and is ready to invest his money more sensibly.

Step One: He decides that although he may want to invest in real estate sometime in the future, he doesn't have enough money yet, and therefore he should restrict his investments to stocks and interest-earning securities. Griese decides that 60 percent of his $25,000, or $15,000, should be invested in stocks, and 40 percent, or $10,000, should be invested in interest-earning securities.

Step One: Deciding on Proportion to Be Invested in Each Category

Method of Ownership	Investment Category		
	Stock	Interest-Earning	Real Estate
Direct Ownership			
	60% ($15,000)	40% ($10,000)	0%
Indirect Ownership (Mutual Fund/ Partnership)			

Step Two: Because his portfolio isn't yet very large, although he fully expects it will be eventually, he plans to invest most of his money in mutual funds. Nevertheless, he wants to become familiar with "direct" investing as well, so, as indicated in the Step Two diagram, he is going to invest $5,000 in stocks and $3,000 in a directly owned interest-earning investment.

Step Three: Griese next needs to decide on the kinds of securities he will purchase within each of the four categories. After some deliberation, he has decided on the investments indicated below.

Step Four: Griese now needs to select specific investments for each of the categories he has decided to invest in. We will leave that up to him, although he, as well as you, might benefit from the suggestions that follow.

Step Two: Deciding How Much to Invest Directly and Indirectly

Method of Ownership	Investment Category	
	Stock	Interest-Earning
Direct Ownership	$5,000	$3,000
Indirect Ownership (Mutual Fund/ Partnership)	$10,000	$7,000
Grand total:	$15,000	$10,000

Step Three: Deciding on Appropriate Kinds of Investments

Method of Ownership	Investment Category	
	Stock	Interest-Earning
Direct Ownership	High-quality growth stock $2,500 Blue chip stock 2,500 Total $5,000	Certificate of deposit $3,000 Total $3,000
Indirect Ownership (Mutual Fund/ Partnership)	Maximum capital-gains fund $3,000 Growth and income fund 5,000 International stock fund 2,000 Total $10,000	Government securities fund $4,000 Corporate bond fund 3,000 Total $7,000
Grand total:	$15,000	$10,000

Here are the "four steps to investment success" described in more detail.

Step One: All too often, investors tend to invest in extremes. Self-employed professionals and small business owners seem to be particularly prone to investing in extremes, perhaps because they think they don't have the time to manage their investments properly. Even though you may think you have a well-balanced and well-diversified portfolio, you may be overlooking some kinds of investments that will help you achieve investment success. Therefore, before you do anything, you need to figure out how much of your total available investments (both now and in the future) should be invested in each of the three major investment categories (as described in Chapter 4): stock, interest-earning investments, and real estate. Some people may not be interested in real estate, in which case the allocation is between stock and interest-earning investments.

Tips—The following guidelines will help determine the best way to allocate (or reallocate) your investments:

■ Before determining an appropriate investment allocation, small business owners and self-employed professionals must first evaluate the risk associated with their businesses. In general, the higher the risk in terms both of the amount of personal capital that is tied up in the business and/or the susceptibility of the business to a slowdown or competitive pressures, the more conservative your personal investment portfolio should be. The following example should help illustrate this important consideration.

EXAMPLE 1: Stanley Steele owns a foundry that supplies castings to a variety of cyclical industries. As he well knows, the health of his business fluctuates with business conditions. When the economy is strong, his business booms, and conversely, weak economic conditions are devastating to smaller foundries in particular. Fortunately, Stanley has survived a couple of recessions, and he well knows that there will probably come a time when he will have to dip into personal resources in order to support his family and, perhaps, the business. Therefore, Stanley quite appropriately invests his portfolio rather conservatively, although he realizes the importance of having at least some stocks in his portfolio as a long-term investment. Moreover, since his business is cyclical, he avoids so-called cyclical stocks because they are likely to suffer at the same time his business suffers.

EXAMPLE 2: Leona Ledger is a self-employed CPA. Over the years she has built up her business to the extent that it is generating an attractive cash flow. She is realistic enough to know that however successful her four-person organization becomes, when she sells it, it will never command enough to provide her with financial security.

Therefore, she is striving to save a sufficient amount of her income from the business to provide enough resources to be able to retire comfortably at retirement age. Leona's business prospects are more predictable and more stable than Stanley's. It is unlikely that the Congress is going to eliminate the income tax, so she will always have a good income from the tax-preparation side of her business. Therefore, her personal investment strategy should not be unlike that of a typical investor with a longer-term investment horizon.

■ Younger and middle-aged people should weight their investments in favor of stocks and, if they are so inclined, real estate because these investments have the best chance of beating inflation and producing good long-term returns. However, some of the portfolio should probably remain conservatively invested. A typical investment allocation for younger people is 40 percent stock, 30 percent interest-earning investments, and 30 percent real estate (excluding the family home). Most people prefer not to invest in real estate. They might choose an allocation of 60 percent stock and 40 percent interest-earning investments or 50 percent–50 percent, which is perfectly okay and a lot easier to remember. Numerous studies of long-term stock and bond performance have indicated that a general portfolio mix of 50 to 60 percent stock and 40 to 50 percent interest-earning investments will provide very good long-term returns without taking too much risk. Of course, your assessment of risk associated with your business, as described in the above examples, may dictate a somewhat heavier weighting of lower-risk interest-earning investments.

■ Pre-retirees who are within about ten years of retirement should begin a gradual shift so that they increase the proportion of their money invested in more conservative securities. This tactic lessens the effects of being caught in a stock market downturn or real estate slump. Younger people have a longer "investment horizon" and can therefore weather the effects of a bear market better. If you, like most independent businesspeople, will need the portfolio to help meet living expenses, an appropriate pre-retirement investment mix might consist of 40 percent stocks and 60 percent interest-earning investments or, if you have real estate investments, 30 percent stock, 20 percent real estate, and 50 percent interest-earning investments.

■ Similarly, when you are retired, the amount of risk you can afford in your portfolio depends upon the extent to which you will have to rely on the funds to meet living expenses. Many retirees, of course, prefer investments that yield current income—either interest-earning securities or dividend-paying stocks. Since you also need capital appreciation to fund a (hopefully) long retirement, you should not abandon stocks entirely. Many retired people find that for the first time in their lives they have sufficient time to devote to stock market investing, and many do quite well at it.

■ If you expect that your income may decline sometime in the future, perhaps by phasing down your business, you should factor that into your savings projections and adjust your plans reasonably and accordingly. Adding risk to your investments to "make up for" expected lower income is not an appropriate course of action.

■ Consider real estate on its economic merits, not its tax merits. For many people, real estate should be a component of a well-balanced portfolio because its long-term performance has been exceptional, although many independent businesspeople often can't risk the illiquidity of real estate investments.

Step Two: The second step involves deciding on how much you want to have invested in "directly owned" securities like stocks and CDs and how much in "indirectly owned" securities like mutual funds. Most investors with small portfolios are best served by indirect investments, which provide diversification and professional management. As a general rule, the larger the portfolio, the larger the proportion that can be invested in directly owned stocks, bonds, and real estate.

Tips—Direct investments have certain advantages and disadvantages. One major advantage is that you have control over the timing of capital gain recognition for tax purposes. In other words, as long as you hold on to a stock, interest-earning security, or real estate investment, you pay no taxes on its appreciation in value. Also, buying interest-earning investments and holding on to them until they mature avoids "interest rate risk," which is the decline in the value of a bond if interest rates rise. Disadvantages of direct investments include the time and expense necessary to manage them effectively, particularly real estate. Also, there is usually less diversification in a portfolio of directly owned securities.

■ Indirect investments, consisting of mutual funds and, in the case of real estate, limited partnerships, have certain advantages and disadvantages as well. Advantages include greater diversification, professional management, and generally lower transaction costs. Disadvantages include the inability to control the timing of capital gains tax realization and, with respect to bond mutual funds, exposure to possible interest rate risk. In spite of the disadvantages, mutual funds belong in every portfolio. In fact, funds play a significant role in the investment strategies of professional investors with very large portfolios.

Step Three: The third step in the investment allocation process breaks down the general categories of investment even further into specific industry, market, or fund categories. For example, if you feel that directly owned interest-earning investments belong in your portfolio, you have many to choose from, including municipal bonds, long-term CDs, Treasury securities, Government National Mortgage Association (GNMA or Ginnie Mae) certificates, and corporate bonds. Assuming, as is invariably the case, that you should also invest indirectly, via interest-earning mutual funds, you might consider, for example, municipal bond funds, corporate bond funds, and government securities funds.

Tips–Be sure to avoid potential conflicts with your own business in selecting categories of investments. For instance, a previous example cited an owner of a cyclical business (a foundry) who wisely avoided investing in cyclical stocks. If the fortunes of your business (an auto dealership, for example) will decline if interest rates rise, avoid investing in companies that will be similarly affected, and opt instead for stocks and interest-earning investments that may benefit from rising interest rates. If you own the real estate that houses your business, you may want to avoid adding real estate in the same city and/or you may want to avoid investing in additional real estate of the same type that your business owns (commercial or industrial).

■ Diversification is crucial. One of the most common mistakes investors make is putting too many eggs into one basket. It doesn't matter if it's a risky basket or a riskless basket. For example, some people are perfectly content putting all of their money in CDs. Over the long run you will suffer without diversification.

Step Four: The final step consists of selecting specific investments within each of the industry or fund categories delineated

---

Bulls make money, and bears make money, but pigs and lambs get slaughtered.

in Step Three—a particular bond or stock or mutual fund, for example. The following rules of thumb will help you select the right investments.

RULES OF THUMB FOR SELECTING INVESTMENTS

You will often be confronted with the pleasure and the dilemma of making investment decisions, including investing any dividend and interest income that is not automatically reinvested, your regular savings, and, perhaps, periodic windfalls, such as a large withdrawal from your business or even the proceeds from the sale of your business. By developing some informal guidelines you can simplify the process of investing— and of monitoring your investments.

Stock investments are best made when stock prices in general are depressed. In other words: *buy low.* A readily available measure of relative stock prices is the price–earnings (P/E) ratio of a major market index such as the Dow Jones Industrial Average. The P/E ratio is computed by dividing the market price of the stock by its earnings per share. A price–earnings ratio well above the historical average may indicate that the stock market is overpriced. For example, the Dow Jones Industrial P/E ratio reached 20 shortly before the October 1987 stock market crash. By way of comparison, the average Dow Jones Industrial P/E ratio over the past several years has been about 14. Investors may want to consider the current price–earnings ratios of the Dow Jones Industrial Average or Standard & Poor's 500 Stock Average in deciding whether or not to invest in stocks. If it is well above the historical average, avoid stocks. If below, consider stocks. The Dow Jones P/E ratio is available in *The Wall Street Journal* and *Barron's*.

Tips–Avoid following the crowd. Buy stocks of good companies that are currently out of favor on Wall Street. Also, participate in their dividend reinvestment programs, which not only automatically reinvest your dividends in more shares but also allow you to buy more shares of the company stock with no commission.

With respect to *interest-earning investments,* you may want to consider the bellwether "yield" on long-term Treasury bonds to judge how high or low interest rates are. Most interest rates move in tandem with the yield on long-term Treasury securities. In recent years, long-term Treasury yields around 9 percent have signaled attractive returns from interest-earning investments (particularly in retirement-oriented accounts). When the long-term Treasury yield exceeds 9 percent, as it has from time to time, you may wish to buy longer-term debt obligations (or longer-term bond funds) to lock in the high interest rates. If interest rates are low, you should buy shorter maturity interest-earning investments like CDs. Yields on interest-earning investments, including Treasury securities, are commonly available in the financial press.

Tip–When Treasury yields are high, pay particular attention to municipal bonds. Over the past several years, tax-exempt "munis" have been offering returns that are especially attractive when compared with the after-tax returns of taxable brethren such as corporate bonds, government-backed securities, and long-term CDs.

Real estate investments are especially difficult to evaluate. Even many experienced stock and bond investors feel intimidated by investing in real estate. Luckily, there are a couple of rules of thumb that can help you assess the financial viability of an investment in income-producing real estate, whether you are buying the property yourself or investing in a limited partnership. The simpler rule involves comparing the total selling price with the current total annual rent income. A property selling for much more than seven times its total annual rent income is likely to yield a negative cash flow. For example, if a duplex selling for $180,000 generates $15,000 in annual rent, it is selling at twelve times annual rental. The rent probably won't cover the mortgage, property taxes, insurance, and all the other costs of being a landlord, so you'll probably have to pour more cash into the investment.

Similarly, if a general partner pays more than seven times gross annual rental to buy a property, the partnership is paying too much unless it can reasonably expect a dramatic increase in the value of the property (if the partnership is planning an immediate condo conversion, for example). Of course, the general partner and, more particularly, the partnership salespeople always expect great things out of the deal although, alas, a less optimistic prognosis would often be more accurate.

Buy stocks when no one else wants them; sell stocks when everyone else wants them.

The key to saving the money necessary to build up your investments: Spend the same amount of money during the three days *after* you receive a major payment as you do during the three days *before* you receive the payment.

The second real estate rule of thumb is to calculate the capitalization rate, usually referred to as the "cap rate." The formula is simple:

$$\text{Capitalization rate} = \frac{\text{Net operating income}}{\text{Total amount invested}}$$

"Total amount invested" includes both the down payment and borrowed money necessary to buy the property. "Net operating income" is total rental income (allowing for vacancies) less all expenses except mortgage payments. For example, a limited partnership in an apartment building requiring a total investment of $3.5 million has an estimated net operating income of $300,000. The cap rate is $300,000/$3.5 million or 8.6 percent. A cap rate of eight or greater is considered desirable. Whether you are investing in real estate yourself or through a limited partnership, make sure the numbers are realistic. A favorite trick of real estate agents and general partners is known as "bumping to market"—raising rent projections from what they currently are to a supposed market level in order to make the deal look more attractive. If you've ever looked for rental property as an investment, you've probably heard the real estate agent say "the rents are this low only because the tenants have been in there so long. All you have to do is evict these old folks and rent the apartments to yuppies." Unless you take great pleasure in evicting elderly people, you should respond, "Tell the current owner to kick them out. When the building is full of tenants paying market rates, I'll be ready to negotiate."

Undeveloped land is particularly difficult to evaluate. Generally, land with significant appreciation potential is well situated

The eventual performance of an investment is inversely related to the enthusiasm exuded by the individual who wants to sell it to you.

and therefore very expensive. Cheap land usually remains cheap. Don't think you've spotted something that everybody else, including all the experts, has overlooked.

Real estate investing continues to be an excellent way to build up wealth, but those who are successful at it share one characteristic—patience. When, based on the above rules of thumb, they find that real estate is overpriced, they are happy to wait until market conditions make a purchase feasible.

Although many independent businesspeople have the skills necessary to purchase, maintain, and manage income-producing real estate investments, they often lack the time and the inclination. Even if you do have the time, avoid making major commitments to income-producing real estate until you gain hands-on experience. Real estate investing can provide marvelous wealth-creation possibilities, but, on the other hand, it can result in mental and fiscal duress instead.

Cash equivalent investments. You may be wondering what you should do with your money if:

1. You think stocks prices are too high, and
2. You think interest rates are too low, and
3. You are either uninterested in real estate or can't find any attractively priced real estate.

You don't have to put the cash in your mattress. Instead, you can park your money in what are known as "cash equivalent" investments, which are really just very-short-term interest-earning investments. Cash equivalents should generally be viewed as a temporary place to invest your money either when market conditions aren't favorable or if you anticipate needing access to some money quickly for personal or business reasons. Cash equivalents include money market funds, Treasury bills, and short-term CDs. Cash equivalent investments should generally be viewed only as temporary because they do not offer any hope of beating inflation by very much after you finish paying taxes on the interest. Nevertheless, there are times when cash equivalents are certainly a preferable investment until stock market, interest rate, and/or real estate conditions become more favorable.

Deciding when to sell. While cash equivalent investments should be sold when you can find a more attractive investment opportunity or when you no longer anticipate needing quick access to cash, deciding when to sell your other investments is a more difficult problem. First of all, you shouldn't make any investment with the intention of selling it within the next few years. One reason you buy high quality stocks, interest-earning investments, and mutual funds is to avoid having to worry all the time about whether or not you should sell them. Nevertheless, you will probably end up investing in some dogs along the way. I use the following rule: If I am disappointed in the performance of the investment over two consecutive years, I'll usually sell it. I define "disappointing" as a stock that does not keep up with the Standard & Poor's 500 Stock Average over two consecutive years and a mutual fund that lags the annual average performance of its category for two consecutive years. In other words, if I own a growth and income mutual fund that underperforms the annual average performance for all growth and income mutual funds for two consecutive years, it's history. Perhaps this rule of thumb means that I will hold on to a lousy investment longer than I should, but I'd rather make that mistake than make the mistake of selling too often. I *know* that selling too often will not work.

PORTFOLIO REDEPLOYMENT

If you follow my suggestion and maintain a relatively fixed proportion of investment in stocks, interest-earning securities, and, perhaps, real estate, you may have to redeploy some of these investments periodically in order to maintain this proportion.

EXAMPLE: Walter Watts, a self-employed electrician, has $40,000 in investments. He invested the money a year ago by placing $20,000 in stock mutual funds and the other $20,000 in a Treasury bill and a couple of bond funds. Over the past year, the stock market has increased rather markedly while the bond market has been so-so. He just summarized his portfolio and found that the stock side had increased to $25,000 in the past year while the bond side is now worth $21,000. So Walter's total portfolio is now $46,000. If, as he should, he wants to maintain a 50 percent–50 percent split between stocks and interest-earning securities, he should sell $2,000 of his stock mutual funds and purchase $2,000 of interest-earning securities to bring him back to an even allocation ($23,000 in stocks and $23,000 in interest-earning

Pond's Law of Investment Return Proportionality:

The rate of return that someone boasts about on a recent investment is equal to the number of losing investments that preceded this "fantastic" investment. For example, if your crony boasts that he just got a 51% return on a hot stock, his previous 51 investments ended up losing money.

investments). Note that by periodically summarizing and, if necessary, redeploying his investments, Walter is forced to "do the right thing." In other words, he sells some of his stock portfolio after it has increased in value (this is "selling high") and buys interest-earning securities after they have experienced a lackluster year ("buying low"). Note also that had stocks declined in value, Walter would have been buying stocks to bring the stock side back up to his desired allocation. Most investors do the opposite; in other words, they buy stocks when they are high and sell them when they are low.

Avoiding investment overload. While you should always keep in mind the need to maintain an appropriately balanced portfolio—one allocated in accordance with your wishes—you don't want to go overboard just because you find market conditions to be irresistible. For example, even if stocks appear "cheap," you may be ill-advised to invest additional money in stocks if you already have a high percentage of your total portfolio in stocks.

WHERE TO GET INVESTMENT ADVICE

Many independent businesspeople are perfectly content making their own investment decisions (they're an independent lot) and can manage very well by using discount brokerage services and no-load mutual funds. Others who have little time and less knowledge and/or a lot of money rely solely or partially on investment advisers. Investments advisers range from commissioned stockbrokers and insurance agents to fee-based investment advisers and managers. I have intentionally omitted another commonly utilized class of investment adviser, usually referred to as the "hot tipster" and normally assuming the role of golf and/or bridge partner.

If you opt to be advised by a stockbroker or other investment professional, you should take time to select an experienced broker who you are comfortable with. I prefer brokers who have been in the business for many years. Since they have survived all kinds of market adversity, they are probably good at what they do. They also probably have numerous accounts and therefore don't have to extract big commissions off my hide to keep food on their tables. Once you sign up a broker, recognize that good advice doesn't always make money, and when it does make money, it may not make a lot. The single most important thing for you to do is to *manage* the relationship. I saw an account a few years ago of a dentist who had given his broker carte blanche trading authorization on a $150,000 account. The result for the dentist: an 80

> *Averaging Down to the Poorhouse:* If your broker urges you to buy more shares of a stock that has lost value in order to "average down," tell him to let you know when the price of the stock reaches zero so that you can buy the whole company for nothing.

percent diminution in value in one year when the market overall was up! The result for the broker: over $20,000 in commissions. No matter how busy you are, you must participate in each investment decision. If you are too busy to do so, you need an experienced investment adviser or manager who will take over the chore of managing your money on a day-to-day basis.

As opposed to stockbrokers, investment advisers and managers may (but not always) alleviate the conflict of interest inherent in broker–client relationships because they are paid either on a fee-for-service basis or as a percentage of assets under management. Unfortunately, you have to have several hundred thousand dollars of investable funds to receive the quality of counsel you deserve. In addition, selection of an investment adviser or manager is no easy task. The first requirement is that the firm be able to accommodate your specific investment objectives. Be sure to check individual performance records through both bull and bear markets. Compare fees, services, size, and investment philosophies of several different companies. Interview the managers. As with any investment decision, it is better to spread your money among two or more investment advisers, but this requires that you have a lot of money in your till. Just as with a broker, once you have made your decision, don't try to second-guess the manager. These relationships *must* be evaluated over a multiyear period. That doesn't mean you don't need to pay attention to them now. Keep informed about your portfolio; in other words, manage your investment manager.

If you want to manage your own investments, there is an abundance of good information that can help you be an effective long-term investor. Most libraries have the *Value Line Investment Survey,* the bible for stock investors, and the *Wiesenberger Investment Companies Service,* the bible for mutual fund investors. *Barron's,* the weekly newspaper for investors, also contains a wealth of timely information. Finally, just reading the business and personal finance section of your local newspaper will help you learn more about investing and current market conditions. Whether you do it yourself, rely on stockbrokers, or do a little of both, take some time to learn more about investing. You will be well rewarded for the effort.

Also, take advantage of your knowledge as a self-employed professional or small business owner by making investments in areas where you have an advantage because of your business and business contacts.

The next section illustrates how you can put together a good long-term investment portfolio that will help you achieve financial security.

PUTTING TOGETHER AN ALL-WEATHER INVESTMENT PORTFOLIO

We've said a lot about structuring an investment portfolio and selecting appropriate investments. Now we can look at how this might be done in real life. Incidentally, the same principles apply to both small and large portfolios, so the following illustrations will take you from a $1,000 portfolio to one in excess of $100,000. All of the illustrations except the last one assume that the investor wants to maintain an allocation of 50 percent stock investments and 50 percent interest-earning investments—which, by the way, isn't a bad split for most of us. The last illustration suggests a lower-risk investment allocation for business owners who may be concerned about the already high risk associated with their businesses.

THE $1,000 PORTFOLIO—JUST THE BEGINNING

What, a $1,000 investment portfolio? Why not? Unless you're some kind of heir, everyone starts at zero (or less). There's no reason why you shouldn't begin to develop good habits by investing your $1,000 in much the way your company's pension manager handles a multimillion-dollar portfolio. The rules are the same.

You can start out by putting $500 into a growth and income stock mutual fund and $500 into a government securities fund. Incidentally, there are many good mutual funds that have investment minimums of $500 or less. Alternatively, you could invest the $1,000 in a "balanced" mutual fund, which consists of both stock and interest-earning securities. The $1,000 portfolio is presented below.

SAMPLE $1,000 Portfolio

Method of Ownership	Investment Category	
	Stock	Interest-Earning
Direct Ownership		
Indirect Ownership (Mutual Fund/ Partnership)	Growth and income fund $500	Government securities fund $500

THE $10,000 PORTFOLIO—PASSING THROUGH

When you have $10,000 to invest, you can begin to expand your horizons somewhat, although you will still probably want to restrict your holdings to mutual funds and, perhaps, a CD. You aren't quite at a level where you can start to make direct investments. But don't fret, because there are a lot of good mutual funds that will help you meet your investment objectives.

As the following diagram shows, you can divide your portfolio among several mutual funds, and the funds will provide diversification as well as professional management of your hard-earned savings.

SAMPLE $10,000 Portfolio

Method of Ownership	Investment Category	
	Stock	Interest-Earning
Direct Ownership		
Indirect Ownership (Mutual Fund/ Partnership)	Aggressive growth fund $2,000 Growth and income fund 3,000 Total $5,000	Government securities fund $3,000 Corporate bond fund 2,000 Total $5,000

THE $100,000 PORTFOLIO—GETTING THERE

Once your portfolio exceeds $20,000 or so, you can begin to make directly owned investments in stock and interest-earning securities. The following diagram shows how a $100,000 portfolio might be structured so that $25,000 is invested in each of the four "boxes," thereby maintaining a 50 percent–50 percent split between total stock investments and total interest-earning investments. The directly owned stocks "box" includes $5,000 in each of five high-quality stocks. Most of the dividend-paying companies you would want to invest in have dividend reinvestment programs. Be sure to participate in them so that your dividend checks can be used to purchase more stocks.

SAMPLE $100,000 Portfolio—50% Stock–50% Interest-Earning

Method of Ownership	Investment Category	
	Stock	Interest-Earning
Direct Ownership	$5,000 in each of five high quality blue chip stocks and growth stocks Total $25,000	CD $5,000 Municipal bonds 10,000 Corporate bonds 10,000 Total $25,000
Indirect Ownership (Mutual Fund/ Partnership)	Aggressive growth fund $5,000 Growth and income fund 10,000 International fund 5,000 Gold fund 5,000 Total $25,000	Government securities fund $10,000 Municipal bond fund 10,000 Corporate bond fund 5,000 Total $25,000

The larger portfolio allows you to invest in a wide range of securities. Note that the stock mutual funds component now includes investments in an international fund and a gold fund.

THE $100,000-PLUS PORTFOLIO—SITTING PRETTY

In addition to making more of the same investments you made for your first $100,000, when your portfolio exceeds $100,000, you can begin to consider a number of additional investments, including: more speculative stocks and stock mutual funds, individual purchases of government securities and mortgage-backed securities, income-producing real estate, undeveloped land, and real estate limited partnerships. Tax-deferred annuities, which are discussed in Chapter 7, may also play a role in a larger portfolio.

A MORE CONSERVATIVE $100,000 PORTFOLIO

The following sample portfolio may be more appropriate if you are concerned about the extent to which your personal

SAMPLE $100,000 Portfolio—30% Stock—70% Interest-Earning

Method of Ownership	Investment Category		
	Stock	Interest-Earning	
Direct Ownership		CDs	$20,000
		Municipal bonds	10,000
		Corporate bonds	5,000
		Total	$35,000
Indirect Ownership (Mutual Fund/ Partnership)	Aggressive growth fund $5,000	Government securities funds	$20,000
	Growth and income fund 20,000	Municipal bond fund	10,000
	International fund 5,000	Corporate bond fund	5,000
	Total $30,000	Total	$35,000

resources (not to mention your time) are tied up in your business, or if you feel the nature of your business is such that your personal investments must be more conservatively invested. The sample portfolio shows a 30 percent stock–70 percent interest-earning investment allocation rather than the previously illustrated 50 percent–50 percent portfolio allocations. You may be surprised to see any stock at all in this portfolio, but you should remember that long-term investors need to have at least a portion of their portfolio invested in stock because of the superior longer-term returns that common stock investments offer.

ON THE ROAD TO INVESTMENT SUCCESS

At this stage, you're probably ready to look over your investments and do what's necessary to put them in order.

First, find out where you stand. Summarize all of your investments. (This may or may not take very long to do.) Your most important investment, your home, if you own one, doesn't count for purposes of this analysis. Be sure to include all funds invested in any retirement plans that require you to control where the funds are invested, such as IRAs and 401(k) plans. An Investment Summary is provided to help you take inventory. Be particularly careful to provide a realistic estimate of the value of your business (Item 5 on the Investment Summary). Just as we often tend to overstate the value of our homes, many owners tend to think their businesses are worth a lot more than they could actually command if sold.

Second, decide what changes, if any, need to be made to your current investments. Are they concentrated too much in a single investment category? If so, you should plan to redeploy the investments to achieve a better-diversified portfolio. Redeployment doesn't need to happen overnight, but start to think about a timetable. An Investment Allocation Analysis is provided to help you plan your redeployment.

Third, begin to invest "new money" according to your overall plan and according to those rules of thumb that will help you achieve your investment objectives. *If you haven't been saving enough, start doing so as soon as possible.*

Finally, review your investments periodically, but not too often. If you make the right investments initially, there is no need to monitor their performance constantly. Most successful individual investors review their investments only once every few months at most.

Investment Summary Work Sheet

This work sheet can be used to facilitate the often laborious process of summarizing your investment portfolio. Date at which market values are indicated: _____

Description	Number of Shares or Face Value	Date Acquired	Original Cost	Current Market Value	Estimated Annual Interest or Dividend
1. Cash equivalent investments:					
Money market funds and accounts					
....	....	....	$........	$.........	$..............
....	....	....	....	....	....
....	....	....	....	....	....
....	....	....	....	....	....
....	....	....	....	....	....
Savings Accounts					
....	....	....	....	....	....
....	....	....	....	....	....
....	....	....	....	....	....
....	....	....	....	....	....
....	....	....	....	....	....
CDs					
....	....	....	....	....	....
....	....	....	....	....	....
....	....	....	....	....	....
....	....	....	....	....	....
....	....	....	....	....	....
Other cash equivalent investments					
....	....	....	....	....	....
....	....	....	....	....	....
Total cash equivalent investments			$.......	$........	$..............
2. Fixed-income investments:					
U.S. government securities					
....	....	....	$.......	$........	$..............
....	....	....	....	....	....
....	....	....	....	....	....
U.S. government securities funds					
....	....	....	....	....	....
....	....	....	....	....	....
....	....	....	....	....	....
Mortgage-backed securities					
....	....	....	....	....	....
....	....	....	....	....	....
....	....	....	....	....	....

Description	Number of Shares or Face Value	Date Acquired	Original Cost	Current Market Value	Estimated Annual Interest or Dividend
Mortgage-backed securities funds					
....	....	....	....	....	....
....	....	....	....	....	....
....	....	....	....	....	....
Corporate bonds					
....	....	....	....	....	....
....	....	....	....	....	....
Corporate bond funds					
....	....	....	....	....	....
....	....	....	....	....	....
....	....	....	....	....	....
Municipal bonds					
....	....	....	....	....	....
....	....	....	....	....	....
Municipal bond funds					
....	....	....	....	....	....
....	....	....	....	....	....
....	....	....	....	....	....
Other fixed-income investments					
....	....	....	....	....	....
Total fixed-income investments			$........	$........	$..............

3. Equity investments:
Common stock in publicly traded companies

			$........	$........	$..............
....	....	....	....	....	....
....	....	....	....	....	....
....	....	....	....	....	....
....	....	....	....	....	....
Stock mutual funds					
....	....	....	....	....	....
....	....	....	....	....	....
....	....	....	....	....	....
Precious metals and precious metals funds					
....	....	....	....	....	....
Other equity investments					
....	....	....	....	....	....
....	....	....	....	....	....
Total equity investments			$........	$........	$..............

Description	Number of Shares or Face Value	Date Acquired	Original Cost	Current Market Value	Estimated Annual Interest or Dividend
4. Real estate investments:					
Undeveloped land					
....	....	....	$.......	$........	$..............
....	....	....	....	....	....
....	....	....	....	....	....
....	....	....	....	....	....
Directly owned, income-producing real estate					
....	....	....	....	....	....
....	....	....	....	....	....
Real estate limited partnerships					
....	....	....	....	....	....
....	....	....	....	....	....
....	....	....	....	....	....
Total real estate investments			$.......	$........	$..............
5. Interests in privately held businesses:					
....	....	....	$.......	$........	$..............
....	....	....	....	....	....
....	....	....	....	....	....
Total interests in privately held businesses			$.......	$........	$..............
Grand total investments			$.......	$........	$..............

If you follow these guidelines, you may end up with a duller portfolio. You won't have much to brag about. Your cronies will probably make you feel inferior because they will go on making high-risk investments that, once in a while, produce a boastworthy return. But the way to win in this business is to devise a reasonable investment program that meets your unique needs and to stick to it. When you're retired, do your cronies a favor and buy them dinner at a nice restaurant. *You'll* be able to afford it.

INVESTMENT ALLOCATION ANALYSIS

Instructions: This work sheet allows you to view the percentage allocation of your total portfolio versus your desired or "target" allocation. Transfer the current market value totals for each investment category from the Investment Summary into the first two columns below. Since the purpose of this analysis is to evaluate the status of investments outside your business, do not include the estimated value of your business. Then calculate the percent of your total investment portfolio in each category. Compare these percentages with your desired portfolio allocation, which can be entered in the right column. This analysis should be prepared at least annually.

Date at which market values are indicated: _____

Current Market Value

Investment Category	Personal Investments	Retirement-Plan Investments*	Total	Percent of Portfolio	Target Percent of Portfolio
Stock	$.....	$.....	$.....	.....%	.....%
Interest-earning investments	.....	.....	.....	.....	.....
Real estate	.....	.....	.....	.....	.....
Grand total	.....	.....	.....	100%	100%

Comments: _____
_____
_____
_____
_____

*List all retirement-plan investments in which you control the investment allocations, including IRA and 401(k) plans.

INVESTMENT MANAGEMENT ACTION PLAN

CURRENT STATUS

Needs Action / *Okay or Not Applicable*

☐ ☐ 1. Summarize all your investments, including any retirement plan investments that you manage.

Needs Action	*Okay or Not Applicable*	
☐	☐	2. Determine how your investments are allocated, in total, among the three investment categories: stock, interest-earning, and real estate.
☐	☐	3. Evaluate the risks associated with your business so that you can determine the amount of risk you can assume in your personal investment portfolio. In general, the higher the risk associated with your business, the lower the risk you want in your personal investments.
☐	☐	4. Plan how you are going to redeploy your investments to achieve a more appropriate allocation.
☐	☐	5. Begin, if you haven't already, to save at regular intervals in order to build up your investment portfolio.
☐	☐	6. Spend at least some time learning about investments and the current investment climate.
☐	☐	7. Don't select investments that may conflict with the risks and conditions associated with your business. For example, if rising interest rates will hurt your business, avoid investments that are likely to decline in a rising-interest-rate environment.
☐	☐	8. Review the status of your portfolio periodically.
☐	☐	9. Coordinate your investing with other areas of financial planning, particularly taxes and estate planning, but don't let the desire to save taxes dominate your investing.
☐	☐	10. Recognize that a buy-and-hold strategy is almost always the most beneficial way to manage a personal portfolio.

Needs Action	Okay or Not Applicable	
☐	☐	11. Mutual funds should play a role in every portfolio, preferably no-load funds.
☐	☐	12. While real estate is often a sound long-term investment, never invest in a property that violates general guidelines outlined in the chapter.
☐	☐	13. Select and control your investment advisers carefully.
☐	☐	14. Above all, be consistent in carrying out your investment objectives.

INVESTMENT ALLOCATION PLANNER

It's now time for you to plan how you should allocate your investments just as has been done in the chapter. If you don't yet have any investments, you can still plan for the day when you will, because that day (hopefully) won't be far off.

Method of Ownership	Investment Category		
	Stock	Interest-Earning	Real Estate
Direct Ownership			
Indirect Ownership (Mutual Fund/ Partnership)			

Comments . . . .
. . . .
. . . .

Investment "To Do" List: . . . .
. . . .
. . . .

6

Strategic Planning for Tax Minimization

Figuring out ways to save on taxes is as American as apple pie and baseball. I am perplexed at how obsessed many people are with dreaming up elaborate schemes to avoid paying taxes. The law has consistently upheld this American right. In the words of Judge Learned Hand: "Over and over again courts have said that there is nothing sinister in so arranging one's affairs as to keep taxes as low as possible. Everybody does so, rich or poor; and all do right, for nobody owes any public duty to pay more tax than the law demands; taxes are enforced exactions, not voluntary contributions."

But just because there are legal ways to pay Uncle Sam less, that does not mean those options are always preferable. How many billions of dollars have been invested over the past decade in tax-sheltered limited partnerships that have proven worthless? Tax planning is an important part of personal financial planning, but *it is just one part*. Any investment or financial decision should include an evaluation of its tax ramifications, but none should be regarded solely or even primarily on that basis. There are many cases in which the option that results in a lower cut for Uncle Sam also results in a lower cut for you! Other tax-saving strategies simply aren't worth the effort and/or may end up backfiring.

EXAMPLE: Bill Buildingblock, a contractor, never even knew he had a great-aunt Mae until her estate administrators wrote to inform him that she had left him $20,000. The Buildingblocks were becoming concerned about how they would pay for their children's education, so they figured this money could be used for those costs. I'm not going to let taxes eat up my kids' college tuition, thinks Bill, so he decides to do as several of his friends have done and gift the money to their oldest child, who just turned 14. He knew that by so doing he would not be subject to the "kiddie tax" on this money and the income therefore would be taxed at the son's low rate. At last, the Buildingblocks thought, we're able to shelter some of the income from taxes.

But how much do they save? In fact, they'll be lucky to save $300 per year in taxes, and this strategy could end up backfiring. By transferring the money to the child, the Buildingblocks could end up qualifying for less financial aid than they would had the money been retained in the parents' names, because the financial aid authorities expect the child's resources to be exhausted to pay for college costs but not the parents'. Another potential pitfall is if the child decides to eschew or postpone college. What happens then? They can't get their money back. This may be a particular risk in the Buildingblocks' case because their son Basil has begun attending lectures by the leader of a religious cult, and if he joins, he will have to "release" all of his worldly possessions.

Surprising as it may seem, many people behave like Mr. and Mrs. Buildingblock (but, luckily, few behave like Basil). They tend to go overboard on tax-saving investments, and they often wind up regretting it. These days, tax minimization requires a new way of thinking. For one thing, lower prevailing tax rates make tax savings less of an issue. Tax shelters are not very useful in the current tax environment, since taxes aren't taking the huge bite they did formerly. But taxes still manage to nibble up enough income to be a nuisance. Good tax planning takes a lot of the sting out of the bite. However, good tax planning cannot be accomplished between Thanksgiving and Christmas each year. Good planning requires advance planning.

The purpose of this chapter is to help you identify certain strategies and rules that benefit self-employed professionals and small business owners, many of whom are able to take advantage of a number of special tax breaks. We will also discuss working with tax advisers since many busy independent businesspeople rely too heavily on their tax preparers. While they may provide you with sound advice, tax preparers are obviously not as familiar with your own needs as you are.

If you're so mad about paying so much in income taxes, quit working. Your tax bill will plummet.

TAX ISSUES PERTAINING TO SMALL BUSINESS
OWNERS AND SELF-EMPLOYED PROFESSIONALS

Since you are a business owner you need to be familiar with both business tax matters and personal tax matters. Without getting into a great deal of detail on business-related income taxes, the following should serve as a reminder of certain areas where you may be able to reduce income taxes attributable to your business. It's good to know what expenses are tax-deductible, and to what extent, so that you don't overlook anything in April; but it's usually not good to let deductibility determine how you spend either in your business or personally. In other words, don't let tax considerations cloud your better judgment.

You may incur numerous expenses that are considered deductible ordinary and necessary expenses practicing your profession or conducting your business. Deductible expenses for professionals include the cost of supplies, the expense of operating and maintaining an automobile used in the business, dues paid to professional services, rent paid for office, cost of fuel, light, water, and telephone used in the office, the cost of hiring assistants, and the cost of books, instruments, and equipment when such items have a short useful life. The cost of items with a long useful life, like office furniture and equipment and professional books are not deducted in the year purchased; instead they are depreciated over several years. Expenses incurred in attending business conventions and the cost of subscriptions to professional journals or information services bought in connection with the performance of your business or professional duties are normally deductible as a business expense, and so are contributions to qualified pension plans. You may be allowed a deduction for business entertainment, as long as there is a direct relationship between the expense and the development or expansion of your business.

If you have an office at home, you must be able to prove that you use the area in your home exclusively and on a regular basis either as a place to meet or deal with clients or customers in the normal course of your business or as your principal place of business. Other home office tax rules may limit the amount of deduction you can take.

Many independent businesspeople are discovering the advantage of hiring family members in their businesses. For instance, if your spouse helps with keeping the books or any other duty for the benefit of the company, he or she should be put on the payroll. The compensation paid must be "reasonable" for the IRS to accept the deduction. In essence, this means you should pay the prevailing rate as paid by other employers for the same type of work. In addition to the pay, a variety of other benefits may accrue because of your employing family members, including participation in the Social Security system, participation in the company retirement plan, qualification for an IRA, and insurance benefits.

Finally, remember that a loss incurred in your proprietorship, partnership, or Subchapter S corporation is deducted from other income. Conversely, any net income from your business, unless it is a Subchapter C Corporation, is added to your other income on your personal tax return.

TAX-DEFERRED AND TAX-EXEMPT INVESTMENTS

Tax deferral. Tax deferral, most often in the form of retirement-oriented accounts, is an important tax-advantaged investment alternative for self-employed professionals and small business owners. Many of them are designed to force you to save, or at least strongly discourage you from spending, because money you contribute to them accumulates with no tax liability until it is withdrawn, whereas if you withdraw it prematurely, it incurs stiff penalties. In addition, when you contribute to some of these plans you can deduct the amount you contribute from your current earnings. Chapter 7, which deals with retirement planning, contains explanations of tax-deferred retirement plans and investments. If it's hard to choose between them, don't worry. You can set up as many as you can afford. The one thing you do sacrifice is liquidity, so you really shouldn't put any funds in these accounts that you might need before retirement. Liquidity is often particularly important for independent businesspeople who may need ready access to resources in the event of business cash flow problems. On the other hand, it is also crucial for most independent businesspeople to build up sufficient retirement-earmarked investments. To sum up my feelings on tax-deferred investing, anyone with earned income should establish an individual retirement account (IRA), anyone with any income from self-employment should contribute to a self-employed retirement account such as a Keogh or simplified employee pension (SEP) plan, and anyone whose employer offers a pension plan (your spouse, perhaps) should be sure to participate to the maximum.

With all of the confusion generated by the tax reform of the 1980s (there were seven major pieces of tax legislation enacted during the decade), we often tend to lose sight of the fact that Congress retained intact the one "tax shelter" that, in my experience, has been responsible for the vast majority of family wealth accumulation in this country. We can still buy and hold capital assets free of taxation on the unrealized accretion in value. In English, this means you can buy stock and real estate, and, as long as you hold on to it, you will not pay any capital gains taxes on the increase in its value. You may already understand this because any increase in the value of your business will not be taxed until you sell it. This is one reason why business ownership has made a lot of people very wealthy. Other people accumulate wealth by buying real estate and holding on to it for many, many years, or by buying a lot of common stock and holding on to it for many, many years. Why? Because, in the instance of real estate, they have been able to increase rents and, over time, have reduced operating expenses and reduced, if not eliminated, mortgage payments. In the instance of stocks, these families have invested in blue chip stocks of good companies with strong dividend-paying records (I refer to them as "the Generals," like Electric and Motors), and these companies increase their dividend rates over the years. Mind you, all of this has been enjoyed without any payment of capital gains tax. This is wealth creation at its best, and there is no reason why you can't do the same thing through your business and/or through your personal investments. As the saying goes, "One way to get rich is to look at what rich people do, and do the same thing." While I don't want you to spend like rich people, we will both be delighted if you invest like rich people.

Tax-exempt investments. Tax-exempt investments can still be a smart way to invest, but they are subject to the same principles by which you would evaluate any other investment. Over the past several years, the yield on many long-term tax-exempt bonds has not been much less than the yield offered by

---

An impossible dream: Preparing a tax return without having a single argument with your spouse.

taxable long-term Treasury bonds. When you consider that you don't have to pay federal income tax on the interest, tax-exempt bonds begin to look like a pretty good addition to a diversified investment portfolio. For example, an investor in the 31 percent federal tax bracket would have to earn almost 12 percent on a taxable bond to match an 8 percent tax-exempt yield on an after-tax basis. Single-state municipals (or municipal obligations of Puerto Rico) can provide exemption from both federal and state income taxes. An alternative to buying individual municipal issues is to invest in municipal bond mutual funds and unit investment trusts that offer tax-free compounding, diversification, and professional securities selection for a low price.

Tax-exempt bonds are one of the few alternatives left that protect current income from taxes and are still generally a good investment, but you must be careful to weigh your alternative minimum tax (AMT) position before investing in them. The interest on some municipal bond issues that are used to finance activities not related to the issuing government are subject to the AMT.

WORKING WITH YOUR TAX ADVISER

Do you need a tax adviser? Many of the best-prepared tax returns from the standpoint of accuracy and tax minimization are prepared by the individual taxpayer. Many people don't mind doing their own taxes because they have the time to become informed about tax-saving matters. If your individual tax situation isn't too complicated, there's nothing wrong with doing your own taxes. It will also save you some money that you, in turn, can save.

On the other hand, for many busy independent businesspeople, tax preparation and planning is intimidating, frustrating, and generally unpleasant. The extensive tax reforms of the 1980s have managed to confuse just about everybody, and as soon as you begin to feel you understand the current rules, the Congress is probably going to change them. A good tax adviser can be a lifesaver. He or she will help you minimize your tax bill by keeping you informed of strategies you can use and by knowing how different expenses and income are treated. A good tax adviser will help you stay up-to-date on tax-saving techniques and the latest changes in tax law.

But you have to work with your tax adviser because *only you are fully aware of your financial situation.* Chances are that the same person who prepares your business tax returns also prepares your personal tax returns. Don't let personal tax planning take a backseat to business tax planning. Opportunities for saving taxes exist in both areas. You shouldn't expect your tax adviser to be a miracle worker who can make sense out of an unorganized mass of receipts and forms you give him or her around the first of April. You should organize your records, keep them organized throughout the year, and always keep tax considerations in mind before making any financial transaction. Simplify your tax life and your tax adviser's job as much as you reasonably can. Separate your business records and your personal records. Consolidate investments, keep the best and most complete records you can, and *avoid all sorts of supposed tax shelters*. Keep a notebook handy to record miscellaneous deductible expenses. Remember, tax minimization and tax planning are a year-round process, so expect your adviser to advise you throughout the year, and listen to the advice. A good tax adviser will be available year-round not only to answer your questions but also to review the tax implications of contemplated investments and suggest tax-saving strategies.

Whether you prepare your taxes yourself or have a tax adviser, you will benefit from obtaining IRS publications that pertain to your situation. Check the accompanying list of IRS publications. An Income Tax Return Summary work sheet is also provided to help you monitor your year-to-year income and tax trends.

IRS Publications

These publications, which are available free from the IRS, can be very helpful in understanding income tax matters that pertain to you.

Publication Number	Title
1	Your Rights as a Taxpayer
15	Circular E, Employer's Tax Guide
17	Your Federal Income Tax
54	Tax Guide for U.S. Citizens and Resident Aliens Abroad
334	Tax Guide for Small Business
448	Federal Estate and Gift Taxes
463	Travel, Entertainment, and Gift Expenses
501	Exemptions, Standard Deduction, and Filing Information
502	Medical and Dental Expenses
503	Child and Dependent Care Credit
504	Tax Information for Divorced or Separated Individuals
505	Tax Withholding and Estimated Tax
508	Educational Expenses
510	Excise Taxes
514	Foreign Tax Credit for Individuals
516	Tax Information for U.S. Government Civilian Employees Stationed Abroad
520	Scholarships and Fellowships
521	Moving Expenses
523	Tax Information on Selling Your Home
524	Credit for the Elderly or the Disabled
525	Taxable and Nontaxable Income
526	Charitable Contributions
527	Residential Rental Property
529	Miscellaneous Deductions
530	Tax Information for Homeowners (including Owners of Condominiums and Cooperative Apartments)

Publication Number	Title
533	Self-Employment Tax
534	Depreciation
535	Business Expenses
536	Net Operating Losses
537	Installment Sales
538	Accounting Periods and Methods
541	Tax Information on Partnerships
542	Tax Information on Corporations
544	Sales and Other Dispositions of Assets
545	Interest Expense
547	Nonbusiness Disasters, Casualties, and Thefts
549	Condemnations and Business Casualties and Thefts
550	Investment Income and Expenses
551	Basis of Assets
554	Tax Information for Older Americans
555	Community Property and the Federal Income Tax
556	Examination of Returns, Appeal Rights, and Claims for Refund
559	Tax Information for Survivors, Executors, and Administrators
560	Self-Employed Retirement Plans
561	Determining the Value of Donated Property
564	Mutual Fund Distributions
570	Tax Guide for Individuals in U.S. Possessions
575	Pension and Annuity Income
584	Nonbusiness Disaster, Casualty, and Theft Loss Workbook
586A	The Collection Process (Income Tax Accounts)
587	Business of Your Home
589	Tax Information on S Corporations
590	Individual Retirement Accounts (IRAs)
593	Tax Highlights for U.S. Citizens and Residents Going Abroad
594	The Collection Process (Employment Tax Accounts)
596	Earned Income Credit
901	U.S. Tax Treaties

MASTERING THE TAX GAME

Tax planning isn't just a year-round issue: it's a multiyear issue. Sound tax-saving techniques usually take years of planning and often take years to develop fully. One of the best things about multiyear tax planning is that you eventually learn to avoid making mistakes that you have made in the past. Investing in anything for purely tax-driven motives is a mistake. Letting tax savings get in the way of sound investing and personal financial planning is a mistake.

It doesn't take a big-time commitment to become "tax aware," it just takes commitment, and you're sure to benefit. Remember that "tax aware" doesn't mean "tax driven." The days

INCOME TAX RETURN SUMMARY

This work sheet can be used to record key numbers from your past tax returns. This is a convenient means of monitoring your year-to-year changes in income, deductions, and income tax burden.

	Year					
	.....	.....	.....	.....	.....	.....
Income:						
Wages	$.....	$.....	$.....	$.....	$.....	$.....
Interest	.....	.....	.....	.....	.....	.....
Dividends	.....	.....	.....	.....	.....	.....
Personal business	.....	.....	.....	.....	.....	.....
Capital gains	.....	.....	.....	.....	.....	.....
Pensions	.....	.....	.....	.....	.....	.....
Rents, royalties, partnerships, and trusts	.....	.....	.....	.....	.....	.....
Other	.....	.....	.....	.....	.....	.....
Total income	.....	.....	.....	.....	.....	.....

Note: The following items are not additive; simply indicate the amounts from the appropriate lines on your federal and, in the case of the last line, on your state/local income tax returns:

Total adjustments to income	.....	.....	.....	.....	.....	.....
Total itemized deductions	.....	.....	.....	.....	.....	.....
Taxable income	.....	.....	.....	.....	.....	.....
Federal income tax	.....	.....	.....	.....	.....	.....
State/local income tax	.....	.....	.....	.....	.....	.....

Note: If your business is incorporated, you may want to prepare a similar summary of past corporate tax returns (Form 1120 or 1120S) to monitor year-to-year changes.

---

of tax-motivated transactions have, mercifully, come to an end. In spite of an incredibly complex "Infernal" Revenue Code, you are better off, at least to the extent that you are better off by making investment decisions primarily on the basis of their economic merits. Although you need to be aware of the tax implications of your day-to-day personal and business activities, such activities should no longer be motivated by their impact on your personal tax status.

YEAR-END TAX-SAVING TECHNIQUES

By now you should realize that personal as well as business tax planning is a long-term and ongoing process. However, sometimes things just don't work out the way you've planned them, or you realize it's already November and you haven't started to plan them at all. There are a few tricks you can use at the last minute to help cut your current year's tax bill and start planning the next year in advance. These last-minute efforts cannot take the place of sustained, long-term planning.

■ Since miscellaneous expenses are deductible only to the extent that they exceed 2 percent of your adjusted gross income, you should tally them up before year end to see how close you are to the 2 percent hurdle. Miscellaneous expenses include professional dues, tax preparation fees, unreimbursed employee business expenses, and certain educational costs. To the extent permitted by the regulations, you can either bunch more miscellaneous expenses into the current year or defer them into the next, depending on where you stand. Similarly, you may want to check on whether your taxable income is nearing a higher tax bracket. If so, you should consider deferring income, to the extent permissible, until the next year, when you might be in a lower bracket.

■ Medical expenses above 7.5 percent of adjusted gross income are deductible. Just as with miscellaneous expenses, try to bunch them up. If you're close to exceeding 7.5 percent for one year, pay any outstanding bills and prepay any medical procedures you will be having the next year. If you aren't going to come close to the 7.5 percent floor, on the other hand, put off as many of these expenses as possible because maybe your medical expenses will be higher next year. (Let's hope not.)

■ To a certain extent, you can also control when you receive investment income. One way to defer investment income is to transfer funds from instruments that pay current interest, such as money market funds, into Treasury bills or certificates of deposit that mature within a year or less and that won't pay interest until next year. You also have control of when you realize capital gains and losses on stocks and real estate. You may want to consider realizing capital losses to offset any capital gains in a specific year. In addition, you can use net capital losses in excess of capital gains to offset up to $3,000 of other income on a dollar-for-dollar basis. If you plan to make a large charitable contribution in a year in which you intend to recognize a capital gain in securities, you'll get a double tax benefit by making the gift with the securities, although you may need to consider alternative minimum tax (AMT) consequences. Generally, you get a deduction for the full value of the securities you donate, and you won't owe tax on their appreciation. Speaking of the AMT, you should also try to determine whether you will be subject to the AMT either in the current year or in the next. Since AMT provisions disallow certain itemized deductions and may tax income at a higher rate, AMT liability must be considered before implementing any year-end tax-saving strategies.

Postponing income isn't always a great idea. If you expect to be in a higher tax bracket next year, then you would try to do the opposite—to accelerate earnings into the current year. In order to decide when to receive the income, you generally have to have a pretty good picture of your tax situation for this year and next. Depending on your particular circumstances, as a business owner you may have considerable latitude in the amount of income you earn each year.

■ If you make estimated state income tax payments, rather than paying the last installment in January, you may want to pay it in late December so it can be deducted this year. Make sure your tax deduction will exceed the amount of interest lost by paying early, however. Also, this strategy won't work if you are subject to the AMT this year.

■ At the end of the year 'tis the season to give vent to your charitable impulses. Don't forget that donations of such tangibles as old clothing, furniture, and books are deductible at fair market value. Keep track of any expenses you incur driving your famous chocolate royale pound cake to the church bake sale—your mileage is deductible at 12 cents per mile. Donations of appreciated stock are often even better than cash, since in addition to

---

They say the only things that are certain in life are death and taxes, but at least death doesn't get worse every time the Congress convenes.

your income tax deduction you can avoid paying tax on the capital gain.

■ When you borrow money to invest, any interest you pay on the loan is deductible, but only against investment-related income. If you paid investment interest this year, try to produce enough investment income to offset it. Capital gains count as investment income for this purpose. Talk to your securities broker about bond (or stock) swaps. You may be able to realize a capital loss by selling a security in which you have a loss and then buying a similar one. You must be careful not to buy the same instrument within thirty days of the sale. If you do, the rules would prevent you from taking a tax loss on the sale.

■ Set up separate bank accounts for business, personal, investment, and real estate activities. Interest deductibility depends on your activity. If you use just one bank account, it's hard to tell where the money came from and where it went.

■ Make sure your withheld and estimated taxes will equal or exceed either last year's tax bill or 90 percent of what you'll owe for the current year. If you think you'll come up short, there may still be time to compensate by increasing the amount that is withheld from your company paycheck for the rest of the year.

TAX PLANNING ACTION PLAN

CURRENT STATUS

Needs Action	*Okay or Not Applicable*	
☐	☐	1. Familiarize yourself with the tax advantages available to independent businesspeople.
☐	☐	2. Carefully analyze any investment or transaction that is being recommended to you or that you intend to make primarily on the basis of tax saving.
☐	☐	3. Coordinate your personal income tax planning with your business income tax planning.

Needs Action	*Okay or Not Applicable*	
☐	☐	4. Coordinate your income tax planning with other important personal financial planning areas, including investments and retirement planning.
☐	☐	5. Don't lose sight of the role of "old-fashioned" tax-advantaged investments like tax-exempt bonds and buying and holding stock and real estate.
☐	☐	6. If you may be subject to the alternative minimum tax, you should incorporate AMT considerations in your tax planning.
☐	☐	7. Maintain complete and well-organized income-tax records throughout the year. Your tax record keeping should be coordinated with your personal record keeping system.
☐	☐	8. Effective income-tax planning is both a year-round process and a multiyear process. Spend some time after tax season with your adviser, if applicable, or yourself planning your income tax strategies over the next five years.

Comments: . . . .
. . . .
. . . .
. . . .
. . . .
. . . .

Tax Planning "To Do" List: . . . .
. . . .
. . . .
. . . .
. . . .
. . . .
. . . .

III

PLANNING FOR LATER LIFE

7

Budgeting Wisely for a Comfortable Retirement

RETIREMENT REALITIES

All of the financial planning you do during your working years, from investing wisely to insuring against the unforeseen, helps you on your way to your ultimate financial goal—achieving financial security by the time you retire. Yet retirement planning per se is all too often neglected, particularly by busy independent businesspersons. Even for higher-income people, a secure retirement requires a lifetime of planning. Sadly, many small business owners and self-employed professionals overlook the importance of providing for retirement and end up working beyond their desired retirement age and/or enduring a less than financially comfortable retirement.

Self-employed professionals and small business owners often have difficulty planning for a financially secure retirement.

■ Self-employed people must take the initiative to establish and maintain their own retirement plans. In cases where it is difficult for the business to afford to provide pension benefits for its employees, the owners must accumulate sufficient retirement-related resources outside of the business.

■ Independent businesspeople often have difficulty focusing on their long-term financial needs. They are under constant pres-

129

sure to run their business successfully, and this prevents them from devoting sufficient attention to their own long-term personal financial goals.

■ While many independent businesspeople hope that the eventual sale of their business may provide a nest egg sufficient for retirement, most small businesses and professional practices cannot be sold for a great deal of money. Therefore, the owners must provide for their retirement income needs independent of the business.

■ Independent businesspeople often spend many years building up their businesses at the expense of accumulating personal savings and investments. This means that many independent businesspeople have fewer years in which to accumulate the resources necessary to provide for long-term financial security.

Several other elements affect the retirement planning process for all of us and may well influence the way you plan for your own retirement.

■ Working people in increasing numbers have set very ambitious retirement expectations. First, and for the first time, most of us expect to retire with no diminution in life-style. Previous generations expected to cut back when they retired. No longer. Second, many people aspire to retire early. More and more people are realizing the dream of early retirement, although many end up (or will end up) regretting it.

■ Life expectancy has increased dramatically since the beginning of this century. The notion of letting people retire at 65 was advanced at a time when few working people attained that age. Now, a person who reaches 65 should plan on living another 25 years, and many will live well beyond age 90. This requires a lot of money. You may work for 35 to 40 years during which you will have to accumulate a retirement fund that is large enough to last 25 years or more.

■ Higher inflation (compared to what was experienced before the 1970s) seems to be firmly entrenched in our economy. High inflation makes it tougher to accumulate resources in advance of

---

Success in retirement planning is much like success in your own business. You have to work and sacrifice over a long period of time before achieving success.

retirement, and tougher to maintain an adequate living standard throughout a long retirement.

■ Fiscal pressures on the government and employers mean that working people will have to rely less on Social Security and company pension plans and rely more on personal savings and investments to assure an adequate retirement income.

IT'S NEVER TOO EARLY OR TOO LATE TO START PLANNING FOR RETIREMENT

Don't despair over your retirement prospects. As an independent businessperson, you at least have some control over your financial destiny. This gives you a considerable advantage over many working people or many employees who increasingly risk being laid off or forced into early retirement. However, the earlier you begin planning for retirement, the better. The following example shows just how dramatic the delay in setting aside money for retirement can be.

EXAMPLE: If a 30-year-old saves 10 percent of his or her gross income every year until age 65, the income from that nest egg alone, combined with Social Security, will provide a very comfortable retirement. Retirement plan income, if any, is icing on the cake. If someone waits until age 40 to begin, they have to save between 20 and 25 percent of their income over the next 25 years in order to retire comfortably on nest egg and Social Security alone. If this person waits until age 50 and has no pension benefits, the amount he or she will have to save jumps to more than 50 percent of gross income per year! Since Uncle Sam takes out at least another 25 precent, the 50-year-old would have to live on only one-quarter of his or her income for 15 years in order to accumulate the funds necessary to provide a comfortable retirement. Can't be done.

So the time to start planning for retirement is now. This chapter will show you how to

1. Estimate how much income you will need during retirement
2. Figure out how much you will need to accumulate in order to fund a comfortable retirement
3. Take stock of your progress in meeting your retirement needs
4. Take action to close the gap between the resources you now have and the resources you will eventually need to retire

You can use the checklists and work sheets provided to help you get on the right track.

You really don't need to begin saving for retirement before you reach age 60. At that point, simply save 250 percent of your income each year, and you'll be able to retire comfortably at age 70.

A PRELIMINARY EXAMINATION OF YOUR RETIREMENT PLANNING STATUS

1. *Estimate how much income you will need during retirement.* If you are many years from retirement, estimating your income requirements at retirement age may be of little concern to you now, but you should at least pay some attention to your retirement aspirations. After all, you may well spend over one-third of your life retired. If, on the other hand, you are nearing retirement age, you must begin to think about your retirement life-style, including the all-important decision about where you want to live.

Once you have an idea of how you want to live in retirement, you can estimate your expenses, first in current dollars and then in future, inflated dollars. To maintain the same standard of living in retirement that you enjoyed during your working years, you will need an annual retirement income of approximately 75 percent of the amount you normally *spend* per year during your working years.

EXAMPLE: The Garners are going to retire in a few months. Last year, they had total income of $48,000, but they saved about $8,000 of that. Based on the 75 percent rule of thumb, they will need about $30,000 in their first year of retirement to maintain an equivalent standard of living. (The calculation is as follows: Since they saved $8,000 of their $48,000 income, they *spent* $40,000. Seventy-five percent of $40,000 is $30,000.)

Depending on your circumstances and desires, you may need more or less than 75 percent of your pre-retirement income. If you are like many independent businesspeople and your income and expenses fluctuate from year to year, you may need to determine what is a "normal" level of spending for purposes of making retirement projections. If you are over 50, make some well-thought-out approximations of what your expenses would be if you were to retire today. If you are within 10 to 15 years of retirement, you should put pencil to paper to prepare a detailed retirement living expense budget. As best you can, try to quantify your retirement expenses. Think about how you expect your life-style to change. You will find that some costs decline, including work-related expenses and income taxes (but not dramatically). Social Security withholding taxes drop to zero unless you work part-time. Other costs will increase, including health care (be sure to provide for health insurance) and, if you are so inclined, travel. Many people decide they would like to try alternative housing arrangements—living in a condominium rather than a single-family house, for example. Ideally, any major changes should be undertaken, or at least experienced, before—not dur-ing—retirement. During retirement, when funds are limited, you don't want to realize that a life-style change was not at all what you wanted.

One of the biggest mistakes that people make in planning for their retirement is either ignoring or underestimating the effects of inflation. Even though inflation is much lower now than it was during the double-digit days of 1979–81, it still takes its toll on your purchasing power. Many retirees, in particular, see their purchasing power diminished by inflation since much of their income is either fixed (like many retirement annuities) or lags inflation somewhat (like Social Security). So when you project your retirement expenses, you must first consider inflation from now until you retire, and then you must factor in inflation for all of your retirement years. Now, you might ask, what rate of inflation should one assume? This is a crucial question. If you were retiring around 1970 and you looked at the inflation rate over the 1950 to 1970 period, you may well have guessed that inflation would continue as it had—at around 2 percent per annum! Projecting inflation is a tricky business, but it must be done. Many experts now recommend that people who are mak-ing financial projections assume a future annual rate of inflation of 4 to 5 percent. Some experts think that even higher inflation rates are in the offing. Incidentally, the average annual inflation rate during the 1980s, including the high rates of the early 1980s, was 4.7 percent. I use a rate of 4.5 percent when I make my projections. As the following example shows, inflation can take a heavy toll on purchasing power.

EXAMPLE: Lucas and Laura McCardle turned 50 this year and are now hard at work trying to figure out how much income they will need in order to be able to afford to retire at age 65. They now figure that in order to live like they want to when they retire, they will need $35,000 of income from pensions and personal investments per year (including taxes) in addition to Social Security. Of course, $35,000 would suffice if they were to retire today, but they will need more than that 15 years hence to have the same purchasing power as $35,000 of income today. In fact, at an assumed inflation rate of 4.5 percent, they will need almost $68,000 of income at age 65 in order to enjoy the same life-style that $35,000 fetches today.

2. *Figure out how much you will need to accumulate in order to fund a comfortable retirement.* Once you have estimated how much you expect to spend when you retire, you need to forecast how much you should accumulate personally in addition to estimated Social Security and pension benefits to provide for your needs for the rest of your life. (The so-called three legs of the retirement stool are pension benefits, Social Security, and personal resources. Job-related income can reduce Social Security benefits.) Before making the actual calculations, two important matters must be considered—life expectancy and inflation during your retirement years. Retirees are, happily, living and, hopefully, living happily for many years. But many who retired quite comfortably 20 or so years ago are struggling financially. They simply weren't prepared to fund so many years of retirement during a period of high inflation. So life expectancy and inflation *must* be considered. Whether the thought appeals to you or not, you should plan on living until at least age 90. (The current joint and last survivor life expectancy of a couple who are both age 50 is 39 years! This means that, on average, one spouse will live to be almost age 90.) So if you are going to retire at 65, you will need enough resources to tide you over for at least 25 years. By the way, I'm a strong advocate of spending it all before you and your spouse die, but please don't plan to spend it all before you reach 90.

Inflation exacts a heavy toll on retirees, particularly those whose income consists mainly of fixed annuities and Social Security. We should return to the McCardles, who are preparing retirement projections:

EXAMPLE: In the previous example, the somewhat startled McCardles found out they were going to need an income of $68,000 when they retire at 65 fifteen years hence to have the same purchasing power that $35,000 has today. As if this isn't bad enough, things get worse. Inflation doesn't go away when you retire. When the McCardles reach age 75, they will need about $105,000 (at a 4.5 percent inflation rate) to have the purchasing power that $35,000 had 25 years earlier. Of course, inflation may end up being less than 4.5 percent (inflation affects many retirees *somewhat* less than it does working people since housing and fuel costs which are often reduced in retirement, are major contributors to the inflation rate) . . . but it could be more.

3. *Evaluate your progress in meeting your retirement needs.*
Estimating how much you will need to accumulate by the time
you reach retirement age can be startling. If you are still young,
this amount may seem more like the gross national product of a
small country, but it is probably attainable without enduring a lot
of deprivation. At this point you need to tally up the assets you
already have available that will eventually be used for retirement
purposes. All of your savings (except those earmarked for specific
nonretirement-related purposes, such as savings for the down
payment on a home or savings for educating the kids) will eventually be available to support you during retirement. If you com-
pleted the Personal Balance Sheet in Chapter 1, you have already
summarized the value of your investments. Three caveats: Don't
overestimate the amount you think you can sell your business
for. If the sale of your business is going to be crucial for a
comfortable retirement, consider having it professionally appraised. Second, don't include the value of your home in your
retirement-related assets unless you plan to sell the house and
become a renter when you retire. Finally, don't include the value
of your personal property because it isn't worth anything to
anyone else anyway (unless you have collectibles, which, in
many instances, still don't fetch very much).

As you review your current retirement planning status, there
is one other matter you should consider—housing costs. If you
can be mortgage free or have a very low mortgage by the time
you retire, your living expenses will be considerably lower than if
you remain saddled with a large mortgage or if you rent. As part
of your retirement planning, you should probably strive to be
mortgage free by the time you retire.

4. *Start to close the gap between the resources you now have
and the resources you will need for retirement.* If you have taken
the pains to figure out how much you need to be able to retire in
comfort, you probably realize (if you hadn't already) that you
don't yet have enough money in the kitty to meet your needs. You
should take heart in the fact that very few people achieve financial independence until they are very near retirement age anyway. What is most important now is to make sure you take the
action necessary to meet your financial needs *throughout* your
retirement. The Retirement Planning Work Sheet allows you to
compute the annual savings required in order to accumulate the
resources you will need for retirement.

RETIREMENT PLANNING WORK SHEET

Use this three-part work sheet to forecast the amount of retirement income you will require and to estimate the amount of savings you will have to accumulate to meet your retirement income needs.

I. RETIREMENT EXPENSE FORECASTER

This section helps you approximate the amount of annual retirement income that will allow you to maintain your pre-retirement standard of living. First, the approximate income necessary to maintain current living standard in current dollars is calculated. Then, by reference to future value tables and by using the assumed rate of inflation, you can project this amount to your estimated retirement date.

Current gross annual income[1]	$..........
Minus amount of annual savings[2]	(..........)
Subtotal (the amount you spend currently)[3]	....
Multiplied by 75%[4]	x .75
Equals approximate annual cost (in current dollars) of maintaining your current standard of living, if you were retiring this year	$..........
Multiplied by inflation factor (Refer to Inflation Factor Table below)[5]	x....
Equals approximate annual cost (in future dollars) of maintaining your current standard of living when you retire	$..........

I N F L A T I O N   F A C T O R   T A B L E

Number of Years until Retirement	Factor
5	1.2
10	1.6
15	1.9
20	2.4
25	3.0
30	3.7
35	4.7
40	5.8

Explanations:
1. "Current gross annual income" includes all income from all sources.
2. "Annual savings" includes, in addition to the usual sources of savings, reinvested dividends and capital gains, and any contributions to retirement plans that are taken from your annual income.

3. If your income fluctuates, for purposes of this analysis indicate an average annual level of spending.

4. The 75% multiplier is a general rule of thumb that says, in essence, that a retiree can maintain his/her pre-retirement standard of living by spending roughly 75% of his/her pre-retirement income. Of course, individual circumstances may dictate a higher or lower percentage. Ideally, you should prepare a retirement budget that details expected expenses. You may find a multiplier less than 75% in some circumstances (e.g., low housing costs due to paid-off mortgage) or, in other circumstances, a higher multiplier (for example, extensive travel plans).

5. In order to project retirement expenses to retirement age, current dollar living expenses must be multiplied by a factor to account for inflationary increases. The inflation factor table can be used for that purpose. The assumed long-term inflation rate is 4.5%.

II. RETIREMENT RESOURCES FORECASTER

This section can be used to forecast pension plan, if any, and Social Security benefits at retirement age and then to approximate the aggregate amount of savings/investments that will be needed by retirement age to cover any shortfall between Social Security/pension benefits and your total income needs.

	Current Dollars	Times Inflation Factor[1]	Future (Retirement Age) Dollars
1. Estimated annual living expenses at retirement age (from Part I)			$..........
2. Annual pension income[2]	$...... x	.... =	....
3. Plus annual Social Security benefits (projection at retirement age available from Social Security Administration)[3]	$...... x	.... =	....
4. Subtotal projected pension and Social Security income (add Lines 2 and 3)			....
5. Shortfall (if expenses are greater than income) that must be funded out of personal savings/investments (subtract Line 4 from Line 1)			....
6. Multiplied by 17[4]			....x 17
7. Equals amount of savings/investments in future dollars that need to be accumulated by retirement age to fund retirement[5]			$..........

Explanations:

1. Use inflation factor table for the appropriate calculation.

2. If your company has a pension plan, enter the estimated annual pension income in the appropriate space. If the estimate is expressed in current dollars, the amount should be

multiplied by an inflation factor to approximate benefits in future dollars. If your spouse works for a company that has a pension plan, similar information can be obtained from his or her employer.

3. Social Security estimates are expressed in current dollars and therefore should be adjusted for inflation similar to (2) above.

4. As a general rule of thumb, for every $1,000 of annual income you will need to fund at retirement age, you should have at least $17,000 in savings/investments in order to keep up with inflation. If you plan to retire before age 62, use a factor of 20, rather than 17.

5. You may be dismayed by the magnitude of the amount of personal resources you will need to fund your retirement, which can easily exceed $1 million for younger persons and/or people with minimal pension benefits. Nevertheless, good savings habits combined with the power of compounding can usually close the gap between current resources and eventual needs.

III. RETIREMENT SAVINGS ESTIMATOR

This section can be used to estimate the annual amount of savings required to accumulate the funds necessary to meet your retirement objectives. The amount computed on Line 7 equals the required *first-year* savings. The annual savings should be increased by 5 percent in each succeeding year until you retire.

1. Amount of savings/investments in future dollars
   that need to be accumulated by retirement age
   to fund retirement (from Part II) $.........
2. Minus resources currently available for
   retirement purposes[1] $..........
3. Multiplied by appreciation factor (refer to Annual Appreciation
   Factor Table below)[2]   x ......
4. Equals estimated future value of retirement
   resources currently available
   (multiply Line 2 by Line 3)   (.........)
5. Retirement funds needed by retirement age
   (subtract Line 4 from Line 1)   ....
6. Multiplied by annual savings factor (refer to the Annual Savings
   Factor Table below)[3]   x ......
7. Equals savings needed over the next
   year (multiply Line 5 by Line 6)[4] $........

Annual Appreciation Factor Table		Annual Savings Factor Table	
Number of Years until Retirement	Factor	Number of Years until Retirement	Factor
5	1.4	5	.1513
10	2.1	10	.0558
15	3.0	15	.0274
20	4.2	20	.0151
25	6.1	25	.0088
30	8.8	30	.0054
35	12.6	35	.0034
40	18.0	40	.0022

Explanations:
1. Resources that are currently available typically include the current value of all of your investment-related assets that are not expected to be used before retirement. Include a realistic current value (less any capital gains taxes that would be paid) of your business if you can reasonably expect to sell it and use the proceeds for retirement purposes. Don't include the value of your home unless you expect to sell it to raise money for retirement. Don't include any vested pension benefits if you have already factored them in on Line 2 of Part II of this work sheet.
2. The appreciation factor is used to estimate what your currently available retirement resources will be worth when you retire. The appreciation factor assumes a 7.5 percent *after-tax* rate of appreciation.
3. The annual savings factor computes the amount you will need to save during the next year in order to begin accumulating the retirement fund needed by retirement age as indicated on Line 5. The annual savings factor assumes a 7.5 percent *after-tax* rate of return.
4. The annual savings needed to accumulate your retirement nest egg assumes that you will increase the amount of money you save by 5 percent each year until retirement.

There is no magic behind accumulating the necessary resources for retirement. You can use the investment strategies discussed in Chapters 3, 4, and 5 to learn how to increase savings and invest wisely. Fortunately, the tax regulations still look favorably on company-sponsored retirement plans as well as personal retirement-earmarked investments. Many of these tax-advantaged plans merit your consideration.

TAX-ADVANTAGED RETIREMENT PLANS—UNCLE SAM'S GIFT TO SMALL BUSINESS OWNERS

As a self-employed professional you need to make a decision either now or in the future about whether to establish a retirement plan through your company. The benefits are obvious. Contributions to the retirement plan are tax deductible and retirement plan investments grow tax deferred until they are withdrawn, presumably during retirement. The drawback of company retirement plans—and it can be serious for many small business owners—is the cost. If you have no employees, you should almost without exception establish and fund a retirement plan. You should be setting aside on a regular basis money that is earmarked for retirement, and there is no better way to do so than through a tax-deductible, tax-deferrable retirement plan. If you have employees (other than family members) you have to weigh the benefits to yourself as well as to your employees of establishing a retirement plan, even a modest one, against the company's ability to afford the plan. This is a decision you will need to make, although if you cannot yet afford to provide a retirement plan, you may be able to afford one sometime in the future.

If you cannot provide a company-sponsored pension plan, you should still consider plans or investments, contributions to which are not tax deductible but the income from which is *tax deferred* until retirement: a deferred annuity, for example.

Keep in mind that there is a quid pro quo to making retirement-oriented investments. Your money is generally going to be tied up at least until you reach age 59½. So you need to make sure you will have ready access to some money should the need arise by keeping some investments, at least, outside of your retirement plans. Some critics will tell you that since tax rates are currently much lower than they used to be, the benefits of tax deferral are not sufficient to offset the disadvantage of illiquidity. My feeling is that liquidity is of secondary importance compared with the need for people regularly to put aside money earmarked for retirement. Anyway, the most vocal critics of tax-deferred investing happen to be investment firms and advisers who are losing business as a result of people wisely placing more of their money in retirement-oriented plans.

The following is a brief summary of plans and investment vehicles that can be utilized by self-employed professionals and small business owners to accumulate money for retirement.

Keogh plans are specifically structured to allow self-em-

ployed people—sole proprietors and partners—to set up their own
retirement savings programs. If your business is incorporated,
you can establish a defined benefit or defined-contribution corporate plan that closely resembles the Keogh plans. In fact, Keogh
plans were designed to allow proprietors and partners to enjoy
the same tax and retirement planning benefits that corporate
plans allow. Most Keoghs are set up as defined-contribution
plans, and they can be structured to allow you to contribute, and
deduct, up to 25 percent of your net income from self-employment (actually 20 percent of your income before you make the
contribution) or $30,000, whichever is less. You can tailor the
plan to meet your own needs and resources. If you have employees, you must extend this benefit to them and make contributions at the same percentage-of-income level that you do for
yourself. You have to decide whether you can afford to extend
this valuable benefit to your employees. If you cannot afford to do
so now, you may be able to in the future as your business
prospers.

In some instances a *defined-benefit* Keogh plan may be a
wonderful means of accumulating a substantial retirement nest
egg. Generally, these plans are appropriate for high-income self-
employed people who are over 50 and who have no other employees. A defined-benefit plan can be structured to allow very
high annual tax-deductible contributions, well in excess of the
$30,000 cap on defined-contribution Keoghs. I've seen these
plans work very well for high-income self-employed professionals
and others who have been remiss in setting up a pension plan in
the past and have a lot of "catching up" to do.

Remember that your Keogh plan must be established by
December 31 of the tax year when you want to begin taking the
deduction, even though you can delay making the contribu-
tion(s) until your tax return is filed (including extensions) in the
succeeding year. (If you missed the deadline, but it is not yet
April 15, you can set up a SEP, which is described below.) You
may continue to make contributions to the Keogh plan after
reaching age 70½ as long as you still report self-employment
income.

Simplified employee pension plans. As the name suggests,
simplified employee pension plans (affectionately known as
SEPs, and they're easy to love) are simple to set up, simple to
maintain, and simply wonderful retirement savings vehicles for
self-employed professionals and small business owners. Instead
of maintaining a separate pension plan as is required with a
Keogh, SEP contributions are deposited into your (and, if ap-

plicable, your employees') IRA account(s). You may establish a SEP after the end of the tax year in which you want to begin taking the deduction as long as it is set up and funded before April 15. Generally, the amount you may contribute is 15 percent of your gross self-employment income, up to $30,000 per annum. You can also kick in an IRA contribution on top of the SEP contribution. As with Keoghs, nondiscrimination rules apply if you have employees. Finally, business owners who don't know when to quit working can still contribute to a SEP after age 70½.

A special "salary reduction SEP" is available to certain small businesspeople. As with a 401(k) plan, employees elect to have their contributions deducted from their pay (rather than your making the SEP payments in addition to their salary). You may establish a salary reduction SEP if you have 25 or fewer employees and at least 50 percent of them agree to participate in the salary reduction SEP.

The *401(k) plans,* also called salary reduction plans, are one of the best inventions since thumbs. These plans rely primarily on voluntary employee contributions although you, as an employer, may contribute to them as well. In addition to the benefit of tax deferral on the income from your 401(k) investments, your annual contributions to the plan, which are deducted from your salary, are not reported as income. Therefore, your salary reductions are the equivalent of a tax-deductible contribution. There is, however, an annual cap on these tax-favored contributions (about $8,500 in 1991) that is adjusted for inflation each year. The same limitations apply to the salary reduction SEP described above. These 401(k) plans are well worth your consideration. More and more independent businesspeople have found salary reduction plans to be a relatively low-cost way to provide retirement benefits for their employees as well as themselves. If you want to consider establishing a 401(k) plan, consult with an employee benefits specialist and/or a financial institution (a no-load mutual fund company, for example) regarding the details of establishing and maintaining these plans.

OTHER RETIREMENT SAVINGS PLANS WORTHY OF YOUR CONSIDERATION

INDIVIDUAL RETIREMENT ACCOUNTS

Everyone who has earned income is still eligible to contribute to an IRA and enjoy the benefits of tax deferral. If you qualify for a tax-deductible IRA, it is inexcusable not to make an annual contribution. Unfortunately, as you probably know, many people don't qualify for tax-deductible IRA contributions. Also unfortunately, many people use nondeductibility as an excuse to forgo making any IRA payments. I may be a lone voice in the wilderness, but I think a nondeductible IRA can still play an important role as a retirement savings vehicle. Even though you may already have established a retirement plan for your business, it probably isn't setting aside enough money to assure a comfortable retirement. So if you need to sock away more retirement money, why not do it through an IRA account, ideally at a good no-load mutual fund company? Then use your IRA money to buy some high-quality stock and bond funds, or take the easy way out and buy a "balanced" fund, which contains both stocks and bonds.

DEFERRED ANNUITIES AND CASH-VALUE LIFE INSURANCE

Insurance companies offer a variety of products that have tax-deferred savings features. A deferred annuity is similar to a nondeductible IRA in that earnings on the money in the annuity accumulate tax deferred until withdrawal. Deferred annuities are no different from any other insurance product in that the details of the annuity contract, including fees and commissions, are almost impossible to understand. Choosing the right one for your specific needs can be very difficult. Unfortunately, while there are dramatic differences among annuities in terms of fees, rates of return, and flexibility, few people go to the effort of searching for the right one. Instead, like most insurance products, these are

---

The only way you can live comfortably on Social Security is if you live only one week of each month.

usually sold, not bought. You might want to consider investing in a deferred annuity as part of your retirement savings program, but, because of the complexity and costs associated with them, only after you have taken full advantage of the other tax-advantaged retirement plans described above.

Cash value life insurance comes in many forms including single-premium, universal, and variable. While these policies afford some life insurance protection, they are often used to accumulate tax-deferred savings for retirement. But the cash value of these policies grows slowly during the initial years of ownership because much of your premium is used to cover commissions and administrative costs. Even over the long term, the costs that go to maintain these policies can drag down returns. Therefore, as with deferred annuities, you can often get "more bang for your buck" by investing in other retirement-oriented savings plans.

OTHER MATTERS THAT MAY NEED ATTENTION

ROLLING OVER VESTED PENSION BENEFITS

If you or your spouse ever leave a company in which you have vested pension benefits, by all means roll the benefits over into an individual retirement account (IRA) within the 60-day limit if the employer pays you your vested portion. (If you are in your mid-50s or older, you may also want to consider using 5-year or 10-year averaging in lieu of an IRA rollover. Consult an accountant.) Younger people, in particular, are inclined to view a relatively small check as unimportant for their retirement. Many end up doing something stupid with the money, like buying a car. Not only are they heavily taxed and penalized on their profligacy, they also sacrifice some resources that may be important to their retirement well-being.

CHOOSING BETWEEN A LUMP SUM AND AN ANNUITY

When you get ready to retire, you will probably have to make the decision as to whether you take the lump sum of your pension benefits, which you would then manage yourself to provide retirement income, or purchase an annuity with your lump sum, which will assure you and, if applicable, your spouse with a lifetime income. There may be some advantage to investing the lump sum yourself, but this option must be considered carefully.

If the monthly payments provided by an annuity are not adjusted for inflation (most are not), and if you are confident that you or your investment adviser can invest the lump-sum amount more profitably, then the lump-sum option may be a good choice if it is available. You'll probably be able to generate more income than with the annuity and at the same time cope better with inflation. There may be a serious drawback to taking a lump sum, however. If you or your spouse should incur substantial uninsured medical expenses (e.g., a long-term hospital or nursing home stay) or should otherwise be subject to the claims of creditors or the mismanagement of money that may occur in old age, your lump-sum retirement fund may be jeopardized. In the worst instances, this could seriously erode or altogether wipe out your pension resources. This eventuality must be weighed carefully in deciding on the lump-sum option as opposed to an annuity. Money in an annuity is usually protected from these adverse occurrences. What is the solution? As we have said, nothing in personal financial planning is "either/or." Perhaps a partial lump-sum and partial annuity may be a desirable compromise. If you opt for an annuity, don't necessarily take the first one offered to you. Payout rates on so-called immediate pay annuities vary widely. Shop around for the company that offers the most attractive terms. If you take a lump sum, you have some homework to do as well. You may be able to take advantage of forward averaging to reduce the tax impact of the distribution, or, if you can afford it, you can further postpone taxes on the plan distribution by rolling it over into an IRA. This way, you won't pay tax until you begin withdrawing money from the IRA.

If you are fortunate enough to expect a large annual income from your retirement plans or you expect to take a large lump-sum distribution, you should speak with an income tax professional about your potential exposure to the onerous 15 percent surtax on so-called excess distributions from retirement plans.

Live it up when you're retired. Spend your kids' inheritance. Spread the word (to everyone but my parents!).

MANAGING YOUR RETIREMENT PLAN
INVESTMENTS

Since you are self-employed or a small business owner, you probably are responsible for managing most or all of your retirement plan investments. These investments, like your personal investments, are essential to your long-term financial security and so must be managed wisely. First, you should summarize *all* of your investments periodically: that is, your retirement plan investments and your personal investments. The reason for this is quite simple—you cannot make investment decisions intelligently without knowing the status of all of your investments. The Investment Allocation Analysis work sheet in Chapter 5 will assist you in summarizing your total investment situation. Managing retirement-earmarked investments really isn't any different from managing your other investments. The following suggestions may help you manage your investments prudently.

■ Never invest in extremes. As explained in Chapters 4 and 5, your total investment portfolio should consist of appropriate portions of stock, interest-earning, and, perhaps, real estate investments. If you find most of your investments are concentrated in a single investment category, you are probably either taking too much or too little risk.
■ As you near retirement age, perhaps within ten years of retirement, you should gradually begin to increase the proportion of your total investment portfolio (not just retirement funds) that is invested in more conservative, interest-earning investments. The reason for this is that you have less time to make up for a downturn in the stock market, which, as we all know, happens from time to time. You still need exposure to stocks, however, and this exposure will continue well into your retirement years. Why? As we saw earlier in this chapter, inflation doesn't go away when you retire, and you therefore need the inflation hedge that stocks have provided, and, hopefully, will continue to provide.
■ You can minimize current income taxes somewhat by loading up your retirement plan investments with highly taxed securities and concentrating your personal investments in tax-advantaged securities.

EXAMPLE: Maxine Macintosh, a self-employed computer consultant, has $150,000 in investments—half in her simplified employee pension plan and half in her personal portfolio. She likes to buy and hold stocks, she likes U.S. savings bonds, and she likes both stock and corporate bond mutual funds. Rather than mix up these investments among her SEP plan and her personal portfolio, she should load up the SEP with stock and bond mutual funds and emphasize individually purchased stocks and savings bonds in her personal portfolio. This strategy will minimize the income taxes she will have to pay on her investment income. Although stock and corporate bond mutual funds are highly taxed investments that pass on dividend and interest income and realized capital gains to the investor, this income will not be taxed as long as these investments are in her SEP. On the other hand, individually owned stocks are tax-advantaged insofar as no capital gains are paid until they are sold. Since she likes to buy and hold, she can benefit from keeping these in her personal portfolio and letting them appreciate in value without paying any taxes. Similarly, interest on U.S. savings bonds can accumulate tax free until they mature, so she is quite correct to keep them in her personal portfolio.

EARLY RETIREMENT

Ahhh, early retirement. How many times have you dreamed of early retirement over the past week? Many hardworking self-employed professionals and small business owners look forward to being able to retire early. If you are one of them, you have your financial work cut out for you. Early retirees face a potential double whammy: They have fewer years to accumulate sufficient resources to fund a longer period of retirement. Unless you can sell your business for a handsome sum, personal savings and investments play an even more important role for the early retiree. A couple of rules of thumb to keep in mind: If you would have to rely on your retirement accounts and/or Social Security benefits to meet living expenses before age 65, you may not be able to afford an early retirement. If your income will be fixed, in the form of an annuity, for example, and once you are retired you will not be able to save a generous portion of it to help fund increased future living costs, you may not be able to afford an early retirement.

The above caveats notwithstanding, it is possible to retire early and comfortably. But you need to plan for it far in advance. You also need to be realistic. Many early retirees think they can readily go out and work part-time to supplement their income for a few years. You may be fortunate enough because of your business background and success to be able to do so. On the other hand, good part-time jobs may not be readily available.

After reading this chapter, you may think you won't be able to retire until you're ninety-five. But remember, virtually everything you do to improve and preserve your financial well-being during your working life is helping you prepare for retirement. Many independent businesspeople spend so many years building up their businesses that they get a late start on saving for retirement, and yet they manage quite well. All of the financial hurdles you have or will have to conquer—such as paying off education loans, starting your business, buying a home, and educating the children—have been preparing you for the sacrifices that may be necessary to fund a comfortable retirement. You've succeeded in the past, and you will succeed in your retirement planning. The following Retirement Planning Timetable and Retirement Action Plan will help guide you.

Retirement Planning Timetable

It's never too early to plan for retirement. To prepare for a financially comfortable retirement, you need to take action throughout your working years. The following timetable describes important steps to take at various ages to help you on your way.

DURING ALL WORKING YEARS

1. Make sure you always have adequate and continuous insurance coverage.
2. Roll over any vested pension benefits you or your spouse receive as a result of a job change into an IRA or other tax-deferred retirement plan.
3. Recognize the need to set aside regularly sufficient savings for your retirement needs. This is particularly important if you do not provide a retirement plan through your business.
4. Evaluate the efficacy of providing a retirement plan through your business. If you are the only employee, you should definitely have a Keogh or SEP plan.
5. If you intend to sell your business, be realistic in valuing it and plan several years in advance of its ultimate sale.

BEFORE AGE 40

1. Contribute regularly to an IRA or other retirement-earmarked savings fund.
2. Purchase a home so that by the time you retire, your housing costs will be under control.

AGES 40–49

1. Periodically check with Social Security by requesting and filing Form SSA-7004. You will receive a "Personal Earnings and Benefit Estimate

Statement" to verify that your wages are being properly credited to your account and to prepare your retirement income projections.

2. Analyze personal assets, and work out a plan for funding an adequate retirement income.
3. Actively manage your IRA and other retirement funds with appropriate emphasis on capital gains-oriented investments.
4. Make a will, and review it every three years or when moving to another state. Discuss other estate planning techniques with an experienced estate planning attorney.

AGES 50–59

1. Continue to request your Social Security "Personal Earnings and Benefit Estimate Statement" periodically.
2. Review your status with your company's pension plan regularly, if applicable.
3. Revise your retirement income and expense projections, taking inflation into consideration.
4. Make sure the beneficiary designations on life-insurance policies are appropriate.
5. Start gradually shifting some of your IRA and other retirement-earmarked funds into lower risk investments with more emphasis on yield.
6. Join the American Association of Retired Persons to take advantage of the many sources of information and help that they offer. The address is:

> AARP
> 1909 K Street, N.W.
> Washington D.C. 20049

AGES 60–64

1. If you are contemplating an early retirement, evaluate thoroughly the advantages and disadvantages.
2. Collect the documents necessary to process Social Security benefits:
   - Both spouses' Social Security cards
   - Proof of both spouses' ages
   - Marriage certificate
   - Copy of latest income tax withholding statement (W-2)
3. Before taking any major actions, such as selling a house, weigh the merits of waiting until age 65, when many special breaks are available to the elderly or retired.

4. Determine the status and duration of ongoing financial commitments such as mortgages and loans.
5. Prepare detailed cash flow projections from estimated year of retirement until age 90, taking inflation into consideration.
6. Practice living for a month under the planned retirement income.
7. Consider different retirement locations. If a location other than the present home is chosen, try living there for a while before making the move.

RIGHT BEFORE RETIREMENT

1. Establish what your retirement income will be, and estimate as closely as possible what your retirement costs of living will be.
2. Determine exactly what your pension benefits will be and whether you want to receive them as a lump sum and/or purchase an annuity.
3. Arrange for a continuation of your medical insurance coverage or, if age 65 or over, to supplement Medicare coverage.
4. Register with the Social Security Administration at least three months before retirement.
5. Inquire about possible entitlements to partial pensions from past jobs.

RETIREMENT ACTION PLAN

CURRENT STATUS

Needs Action   *Okay or Not Applicable*

☐ ☐ 1. You must begin to plan for retirement now—it's never too early. Begin by preparing projections of your retirement income and expenses. If you are within ten years of retirement, prepare these projections annually.

☐ ☐ 2. You cannot rely on retirement and Social Security benefits alone to provide for an adequate retirement. Therefore, get into the habit of setting aside each year some money that is earmarked solely for retirement. An IRA (whether or not it is deductible) is an inexpensive and effective means of starting to get into this habit.

Needs Action	Okay or Not Applicable	
☐	☐	3. Consider establishing a retirement plan through your business that is appropriate to your circumstances and needs. You may need to consult with a pension specialist to make sure you adopt the right kind of plan and set it up correctly.
☐	☐	4. If you do not have a retirement plan through your business, recognize that you will need to set aside that much more money personally in order to provide a sufficient retirement income. Consider making tax-deferred investments that can be purchased outside of a company retirement plan, such as IRAs and deferred annuities.
☐	☐	5. One of the best things you can do during your working years to prepare for retirement is to be mortgage free by retirement age. If you are a renter or will still have a large mortgage when you retire, remember that you will need a considerably larger nest egg to cover your housing costs.
☐	☐	6. Review your retirement plan investments periodically. Be sure to consider them in conjunction with your entire investment portfolio, personal investments as well as retirement plan investments.

Comments: . . . .
. . . .
. . . .
. . . .
. . . .
. . . .

Retirement "To Do" List: . . . .
. . . .
. . . .
. . . .
. . . .

8

Planning Your Estate for the Here and Now as Well as the Hereafter

Estate planning is hardly the most exciting topic to discuss. You may think estate planning is only for the very wealthy or the very dead. Actually, every adult, married or single, rich or not-so-rich, needs to pay some attention to estate planning. Most of us don't like to think about estate planning, for a couple of reasons. First, since you should invariably involve attorneys in helping you with your estate plans, you're likely to run across some complicated and confusing terminology, such as *intestacy* (sounds like someone who is missing some organs), *codicil* (sounds like a fish), *buy–sell agreement* (sounds like what your stockbroker tries to do every day with your investments), *QTIP trust* (sounds like a trust you put in your ear), and *durable power of attorney* (sounds like you're authorizing your lawyer to send you bills for the rest of your life). The second reason is that estate planning invariably forces us to think about our own mortality. While they say "only the good die young," and that may assure you a long life, the fact is that no one has yet lived forever.

What is estate planning? It is the process of organizing your financial and personal interests, in accordance with prevailing laws, so that *your* wishes are met with a minimum of inconvenience to your family. Estate planning can also assure that your estate incurs the minimum possible estate tax burden. This chapter explains, in English, how you can develop a "bare bones" estate plan if that's all you need, and also provides some information on more elaborate techniques that may interest you now or sometime in the future. Finally, it contains some tips for you if you are approaching your golden years, or for caring for your parents' financial planning concerns if they are. Effective estate planning need not be complicated, and it has several worthwhile objectives, including

■ Minimizing the problems and expenses of probate; avoiding potential family conflicts, where possible
■ Providing your spouse with as much responsibility and flexibility in estate management as desired, consistent with potential tax savings
■ Providing for the conservation of your estate and its effective management following death of either or both spouses
■ Minimizing taxes at time of death as well as income taxes after death
■ Avoiding leaving the children "too much too soon"
■ Planning for the orderly disposition of your business in the event of your death
■ Providing for adequate liquidity to cover taxes and other expenses at death without the necessity of forced sale of assets
■ Providing for estate management in event of incapacity of either spouse
■ Coordinating your personal estate plan with all business arrangements, if applicable
■ Organizing all important papers affecting your estate plan in a spot known to all family members, and reviewing them at least annually
■ Informing all family members about the overall estate plan

Self-employed professionals and small business owners should be cognizant of several issues that may affect their estate planning. Estate planning for independent businesspeople is usually more complex, and in some instances can be very complex. The main reason for this is that the estate planning must consider a plethora of matters pertaining to the business, including providing for successor management or the orderly sale or liquidation of the business and providing sufficient estate liquidity to cover the survivors' immediate needs and estate taxes.

In spite of the need for estate planning, many independent

businesspeople are too busy and/or not sufficiently informed to prepare even the minimum estate planning documents or, once prepared, to keep them up-to-date.

Another matter that may affect the estate planning of small business owners is the appropriate way to pass the business on to family members if this is desired during your lifetime or assessing the ability of the family to continue the business (as well as their ability to manage a possibly large estate outside of the business) upon your death.

Self-employed people often accumulate larger estates that can benefit from more advanced estate planning techniques. These techniques not only maximize the amount that can be transferred to the next generation, they also can provide certain benefits during your lifetime.

I'm a strong advocate of spending it all before you die (if you have children, you've already done enough for them), but chances are that in spite of your best efforts to follow my recommendation you will end your days with some money left over. Depending on how much is likely to be left over and your specific wishes as to the disposition of your estate, you at least need to have some basic estate planning documents prepared. Many self-employed professionals and small business owners will benefit from some of the optional extras as well.

EXAMPLE: William and Wilma Nowill were a typical family, two children in grammar school, two cars, one house, one mortgage, and no wills. Will owned a printing business, and Wilma was a free-lance writer. Of course, they knew that it was important to have wills, and they intended to get around to it someday. Will died suddenly. Fortunately, he had some life insurance and a few investments that Wilma thought would be sufficient to tide them over for a while until the business, by far their most important asset, could be sold. She figured their situation was so typical that she would receive all of the estate, just as they had intended to do in their wills. But such was not the case. The "laws of intestate distribution" for her state are not unlike many others. Wilma's share of Will's estate is only *one-third*. The other two-thirds goes to the children, and the court must appoint someone to oversee the children's inheritance because they are minors. So, although Wilma had a serious need for the entire inheritance, she is out of luck. Also, the court will appoint an administrator to carry out the duties of settling Will's estate, which can be much more

Two things in life are certainties: death and taxes. Unfortunately, death, unlike taxes, cannot be postponed by filing an extension.

costly than if an executor had been appointed in a will. To make matters worse, they had not planned for the disposition of Will's printing business so it is now in jeopardy because Wilma can't afford to keep it running in the absence of her husband. Amidst all this chaos, Wilma had better get a will right away because if she now dies (or if they had died in a common accident), the courts would also appoint guardians for the children because they had not been designated in a will.

ESTATE PLANNING PROBLEMS OF BUSINESS OWNERS

Before getting into a discussion of minimum estate planning needs as well as some more advanced techinques that may be appropriate for you, we should first explore the many estate planning problems that you may have to confront as a result of owning a business. Planning these matters while you are in good health is crucial, and it allows you to address two important issues simultaneously. First, you need to be planning for the disposition of your business during your lifetime because you presumably don't want to work forever. At the same time, this planning can address the disposition of your business in the event you die while still owning and operating it. These issues require a lot of thought and you will eventually need to seek the advice of an attorney and, perhaps, an accountant who are well versed in lifetime and estate planning for small business owners. The way you approach planning for the disposition of your business depends in part on the form of business ownership—in other words, whether it is a sole proprietorship, partnership, or corporation. Generally, corporations and partnerships are easier to deal with from the standpoint of transferring ownership of the business either during your lifetime or after your death.

Depending on your individual circumstances, you may need to address any of the following as they relate to your estate planning for your business. All too many self-employed professionals and small business owners neglect to attend to these important matters, which, as you can imagine, could well leave their family members and other survivors in a very difficult position.

- Planning for disposing of the business in the event of death or a designation of successor management.
- Building a so-called "second estate" if the business is unlikely to provide adequate resources upon its disposition.
- Assuring that there is sufficient cash on hand to continue business operations in the event of your demise.

- Structuring arrangements to sell your interest in the business either to other partners, to shareholders, or to key employees.
- If the business is to be kept in the family, deciding on the best way to transfer the business to other family members who will fill key positions.
- Preparing projections of the estate tax implications of a business disposition and providing for sufficient resources to assure that estate taxes can be paid when due. Estate taxes can be paid in installments when the business represents a substantial portion of the deceased's estate.
- Providing sufficient estate liquidity to meet the needs of family members during the period after your demise.
- Considering the use of irrevocable life insurance trusts, key person life insurance, disability income insurance, and overhead insurance to provide adequate resources in the event of your disability or death.

The importance of dealing with these matters now cannot be overemphasized. Chances are that your business represents your most important asset and that its ultimate success is seriously jeopardized in the event of your absence. Just as with all other facets of estate planning, these issues are very discomfiting to address. By doing so in the context of your estate planning, you are also, at the same time, forced to think about what you eventually are going to do with the business during your lifetime because, chances are, thank heavens, that you will live to see your business change hands.

The next section deals with basic and essential estate planning documents.

MINIMUM ESTATE PLANNING NEEDS

Estate planning need not be complicated to be effective. A simple estate plan will save legal fees and unnecessary delays and ensure that your estate is distributed in accordance with your wishes. It may also have some positive effects while you are still alive. Unless you want to leave your family in chaos after your demise, take the following minimum steps to provide your loved ones, and yourself, some peace of mind. Single people need to plan their estates as well because it is highly unlikely these will be distributed in accordance with their wishes upon their demise. For example, many single people want to leave at least a portion of their estates to charity, yet if they die intestate, the charity will never see any of that money. A minimum estate plan usually consists of four documents.

1. *Valid and up-to-date will.* Everyone knows the importance of preparing and maintaining a will. Yet the vast majority of adults do not have wills. Your will should specify exactly how your estate is to be divided. It should be drawn up by an experienced attorney. As the above example shows, intestate estates (meaning dying without a will) incur higher than necessary legal fees and unnecessary delays—and a judge, rather than you, will decide how your estate is to be distributed. Changing your will to reflect changes in your personal circumstances (including moving to another state) or in state and federal laws is also essential—and often overlooked. Writing a will is simple, but it's not foolproof.

EXAMPLE: *A Simple Will Can Be an Expensive ($235,000) Mistake*
Bad idea: The garden variety will, which, in essence, says "all to my spouse," could end up costing your children or other heirs a lot of money. Assume a husband has an estate of $1.2 million (which, by the way, is by no means an unusually large estate for older persons), and he dies leaving all of it to his wife. No federal estate taxes are owed because the transfer qualifies for the unlimited marital deduction. But what if the wife dies right after the husband? She's got at least $1.2 million to bequeath but has only the $600,000 tax-free exemption available to reduce estate taxes. Her taxable estate, therefore, is $600,000 (the $1.2 million gross estate minus the $600,000 exemption). The federal estate tax on this $600,000 is a whopping $235,000 which could have been avoided altogether with some modest estate planning.

Better idea: The husband should limit the wife's taxable estate to the amount covered by her $600,000 exemption by not willing everything he owns to her. He can do this by allowing her the full use of all of the property to meet her needs but putting a part of his estate in a trust for her that will not be subject to estate tax at her death.

Of course, the wife might die first, but the estate can be structured to avoid some or all estate taxes no matter who dies first. In the above example, the husband can, during his lifetime, give his wife $600,000 (there are no gift taxes on transfers to a spouse), and she could leave that to him in her will to use if he survives her. Incidentally, these arrangements go under a variety of monikers, including "marital trusts," "A-B trusts," "power of appointment trusts," and (are you ready for this one?) "qualified terminable interest property (QTIP) trusts."

This is but one example of the myriad of estate planning opportunities available even to those who somehow missed making the "*Forbes* 400 Richest Americans" list.

Whether you have a will or not (but know you should), the Will Planning/Review Checklist covers important considerations pertaining to the preparation or periodic review of a will.

WILL PLANNING/REVIEW CHECKLIST

This checklist can be used either to plan a new will or review an existing will.

Yes	No	Unsure	N/A	
☐	☐	☐	☐	1. If there is an existing will, does it reflect the current situation, including birth of heirs and changes in the tax laws, and not contain obsolete sections, including state or residence and executor suitability?
☐	☐	☐	☐	2. Will any specific bequests or legacies be made?
☐	☐	☐	☐	3. Are there any bequests to charity, either outright or in trust, in order to obtain benefit of the charitable deduction?
☐	☐	☐	☐	4. Has the disposition of personal property, furniture, jewelry, and automobiles, for example, been planned?
☐	☐	☐	☐	5. Has provision been made for the disposition of real estate?
☐	☐	☐	☐	6. Does the will provide direction for the disposition or transfer of ownership of a family business?
☐	☐	☐	☐	7. Does the will provide for the disposition of property if an heir predeceases?
☐	☐	☐	☐	8. Will trusts be established for certain beneficiaries, or will they receive the assets outright?
☐	☐	☐	☐	9. Will certain beneficiaries be provided with periodic payments of income?
☐	☐	☐	☐	10. Does the will take advantage of the unlimited marital deduction to the most effective and practical extent allowed?
☐	☐	☐	☐	11. Has consideration been given to providing for marital and nonmarital trusts in the will?
☐	☐	☐	☐	12. Is the custody of minors satisfactorily addressed?

Current Status

Current Status				
Yes	No	Unsure	N/A	
☐	☐	☐	☐	13. Has consideration been given to appointing a "financial" guardian for the children in addition to a "personal" guardian?
☐	☐	☐	☐	14. Does the will specify that any minor beneficiary's share of the estate will be held until he reaches maturity?
☐	☐	☐	☐	15. Does the will provide for a guardianship or trust to protect the inheritance of disabled or incompetent beneficiaries?
☐	☐	☐	☐	16. Have provisions been made to dispose of business interests?
☐	☐	☐	☐	17. Have appropriate and capable persons or institutions been appointed to serve as executor, trustee, and/or guardian?
☐	☐	☐	☐	18. Does the will name an alternate or successor executor, trustee, and/or guardian?
☐	☐	☐	☐	19. Should any special powers be given to or taken away from the executor?
☐	☐	☐	☐	20. Has the executor's bond requirement been waived?
☐	☐	☐	☐	21. Are specific powers granted to the executor, as necessary, such as to retain or sell property, to invest trust and estate assets, to allocate receipts and disbursements to income and principal, to make loans and borrow funds, or to settle claims?
☐	☐	☐	☐	22. Is the ownership of the assets complementary to the provisions of the will (i.e., some assets may pass outside of the will by contract or by type of ownership)?
☐	☐	☐	☐	23. Does the will state who will receive property if the beneficiary disclaims it? (Disclaimers can be an effective postmortem planning device.)
☐	☐	☐	☐	24. Have any special directions for the funeral or memorial been provided?

Yes	No	Unsure	N/A	
☐	☐	☐	☐	25. Have sources been identified from which debts, funeral expenses, and estate administrative costs will be paid?
☐	☐	☐	☐	26. Will the survivors have enough cash to pay ordinary family living expenses while the estate is in probate?

Current Status

An experienced lawyer can help you draw up a will to specify exactly how you want your estate divided. Your will does not prevent you from doing whatever you like with your property while you're still alive, and if your circumstances change, you can always write a new one.

2. *Durable power of attorney.* As if death isn't bad enough to contemplate, the second essential estate planning document will become indispensable in the event you become incapacitated and unable to manage your financial affairs because of an accident, illness, or age, your right to do so may be revoked by a court order and a guardian will be appointed. It is possible that the court will not appoint the guardian you would have chosen, and the difficulties in securing court approval of the guardian's actions will create undue red tape and confusion. There are basically two ways to protect personal assets and ensure they will continue to be managed as you see fit. You can appoint a guardian for yourself by assigning a durable power of attorney, or you can establish a living trust.

Assigning a durable power of attorney ensures that if you ever become unable to manage your own financial and personal affairs, someone you trust will be able to act on your behalf. A power of attorney may be either special, applying to only certain situations, or general, giving the attorney-in-fact virtually limitless control over the principal (the person who created the arrangement). General powers of attorney should be avoided as they are dangerous, subject to abuse, and usually unnecessary.

A power of attorney may also be either indefinite or for a specific length of time. No matter how it is assigned, it may be canceled at any time, and it terminates immediately upon the death of the principal. Your state may not recognize durable powers of attorney. If so, you can use a living trust to protect you in the event of incapacity. Since living trusts can accomplish more than a durable power of attorney, you may want to consider a living trust in lieu of a durable power. They are discussed in the "Trusts" section, below.

Also, consider appointing a "financial" guardian in addition to a "personal" guardian for your children in order to separate the responsibility of managing your child's finances from the responsibility of raising your child. This may be particularly desirable if you have a large estate.

3. *Living will*. Now that we've taken care of your death and incapacity, we can move on to another dismal topic, terminal illness. You are probably aware of the medical dilemmas surrounding terminally ill patients and the importance of trying to accommodate the patient's wishes. If you are concerned about these matters personally, you should consider drafting a so-called living will, informing family members and physicians that under certain circumstances you do not wish to be kept alive by artificial means. You get to define the circumstances. Living wills are legally recognized in most states, and even where they are not, experts suggest that preparing one anyway can be very helpful if, and when, the need to make these difficult decisions arises.

4. *Letter of instructions*. A letter of instructions is not as crucial as other essential estate planning documents, but you will be doing your heirs a big favor by preparing one. A letter of instructions is an informal document (you don't need an attorney to prepare it) that gives your survivors information concerning important financial and personal matters. Although it does not carry the legal weight of a will, the letter of instructions is very important because it clarifies any further requests to be carried out upon death and provides essential financial information, thus relieving the surviving family members of needless worry and speculation. The Letter of Instructions Checklist will help you decide what to include.

Obviously, your survivors will benefit if you prepare a letter of instructions. But you will too, insofar as a well-prepared letter of instructions is a great way to organize your personal records. Be sure to keep it up-to-date since the information contained therein is likely to change. Finally, make sure your heirs know where the letter is, before they ever need it. Perhaps you should tape it to your refrigerator door so everyone will know where it is located.

LETTER OF INSTRUCTIONS CHECKLIST

It's really up to you what you want to put in your letter of instructions. Since a letter of instructions is not a legal document like a will, you have a lot more leeway in both the language and content. Your letter is a good place to put personal wishes and final comments, but your heirs will be very grateful if you include some more useful information. The following is a list of suggestions for what to put in your letter of instructions. Even if you're not planning to die in the near future, preparing a letter of instructions is a good way to start getting your records in order. Your heirs will also be very grateful.

☐ *FIRST THINGS TO DO*
- Acquaintances and organizations to be called, including Social Security, the bank, your clients
- Arrangements to be made with funeral home
- Lawyer's name and telephone
- Newspapers to receive obituary information
- Location of insurance policies

☐ *CEMETERY AND FUNERAL*
- Details of your wishes and any arrangements you have made

☐ *FACTS FOR FUNERAL DIRECTOR*
- Vital statistics, including your full name, residence, marital status, spouse's name, date of birth, birthplace, father's and mother's names and birthplaces, length of residence in state and in United States, military records/history, Social Security number, occupation, and life insurance information

☐ *INFORMATION FOR DEATH CERTIFICATE AND FILING FOR BENEFITS*
- Citizen of, race, marital status, name of next of kin (other than spouse), relationship, address, and birthplace

☐ *EXPECTED DEATH BENEFITS*
- Information about any potential death benefits (including life insurance, profit sharing, pension plan, or accident insurance), life insurance companies, Social Security, the Department of Veterans Affairs, or any other source

☐ *SPECIAL WISHES*
- Anything you want them to know

☐ *PERSONAL EFFECTS*
- A list of who is to receive certain personal effects

☐ *PERSONAL PAPERS*
- Locations of important personal documents, including your will, birth and baptismal certificates, communion and confirmation certificates, diplomas, marriage certificate, military records, naturalization papers, and any other documents (e.g., adoption, divorce)

☐ *SAFE-DEPOSIT BOX**
- Location and number of box and key and an inventory of contents

☐ *POST OFFICE BOX*
- Location and number of box and key (or combination)

☐ *INCOME TAX RETURNS*
- Location of all previous returns
- Location of your estimated tax file
- Tax preparer's name

☐ *LOANS OUTSTANDING*
- Information for loans other than mortgages, including bank name and address, name on loan, account number, monthly payment, location of papers and payment book, collateral, and information on any life insurance on the loan

☐ *DEBTS OWED TO THE ESTATE*
- Debtor, description, terms, balance, location of documents, and comments on loan status/discharge

☐ *SOCIAL SECURITY*
- Full name, SS number, and the location of Social Security card

☐ *LIFE INSURANCE*
- Policy numbers and amounts, location of policy, whose life is insured, insurer's name and address, kind of policy, beneficiaries, issue and maturity date, payment options, and any special facts

☐ *VETERANS*
- If you are a veteran, give information on collecting benefits from local Veterans Affairs office

☐ *OTHER INSURANCE*
- If any other insurance benefits or policies are in force, including accident, homeowner's/renter's, automobile, disability, medical, personal or professional liability, give insurer's name and address, policy number, beneficiary, coverage, location of policy, term, how acquired (if through professional or other group), agent

---

*State law may require the bank to seal the deceased's box as soon as notified of his or her death, even if the box is jointly owned.

□ *INVESTMENTS*
- Stocks: company, name on certificates, number of shares, certificate numbers, purchase price and date, and location of certificates
- Bonds/notes/bills: Issuer, issued to, face amount, bond number, purchase price and date, maturity date, and location of certificates
- Mutual funds: company, name on account, number of shares or units, and location of statements and certificates
- Other investments: for each investment, list amount invested, to whom issued, maturity date, issuer, and other applicable data, and location of certificates and other vital papers

□ *FAMILY BUSINESS*
- Description of plans that have already been made to provide for business disposition or succession
- Suggestions to assure that the business will be able to continue to operate as smoothly as possible immediately after death; the less the survivors are involved in the business, the more details should be provided as to its operation

□ *HOUSEHOLD CONTENTS*
- List of contents with name of owners, form of ownership, and location of documents, inventory, and appraisals

□ *AUTOMOBILES*
- For each car: year, make, model, color, identification number, title in name(s) of, and location of title and registration

□ *IMPORTANT WARRANTIES, RECEIPTS*
- Location and description

□ *DOCTORS' NAMES, ADDRESSES, AND TELEPHONES*
- Including dentist, children's pediatrician, and children's dentist

□ *CHECKING ACCOUNTS*
- Name of bank, name on account, account number, and location of passbook (or receipt) for all accounts

□ *CREDIT CARDS*
- For each card: company (including telephone and address), name on card, number, and location of card

□ *HOUSE, CONDO, OR CO-OP*
- About the home: in whose name, address, legal description, other descriptions needed, lawyer at closing, and locations of statement of closing, policy of title insurance, deed, and land survey
- About the mortgage: held by, amount of original mortgage, date taken out, amount owed now, method of payment, and location of payment book, if any (or payment statements)

- About life insurance on mortgage: policy number, location of policy, and annual amount
- About property taxes: amount and location of receipts
- About the cost of house: initial buying price, purchase closing fee, other buying costs (real estate agent, legal, taxes), and home improvements
- About improvements: what each consisted of, cost, date, and location of bills
- For renters: lease location and expiration date

☐ *FUNERAL PREFERENCES*
- Specify whether *or not* you would like to have any of the following done: Donate organs, autopsy if requested, simple arrangements, embalming, public viewing, least expensive burial or cremation container, or immediate disposition. Remains should be: donated (details of arrangements made), cremated (and the ashes: scattered, buried at), disposed of as follows (details), or buried (at)
- Specify which of the following services should be performed: memorial (after disposition), funeral (before disposition), or graveside to be held at: church, mortuary, or other
- Specify where memorial gifts should be given or whether or not to omit flowers
- If prearrangements have been made with a mortuary, give details

☐ *SIGNATURE AND DATE*

The four documents described above—a will, durable power of attorney, a living will, and a letter of instructions—are the essential components of a basic estate plan. You may well be able to benefit from other estate planning techniques, including trusts, gifts to relatives, and selecting the appropriate form of property ownership.

OPTIONAL EXTRAS THAT CAN BENEFIT YOU IN THE HERE AND NOW (AS WELL AS THE HEREAFTER)

You may be fortunate enough to accumulate a sizable estate. Generally, if your estate is expected to be close to or in excess of $1 million, you may benefit from some of the estate planning

> It's 10:00 P.M. . . . Do your heirs know where your letter of instructions is?

techiques described below. This may seem like a king's ransom at this point in your life, but if you project your estate into the future, you may well achieve these lofty levels. How, you might ask, can you figure out the current size of your estate? The following diagram will allow you to make a quick, albeit rough, estimate of the value of your estate.

QUICK ESTIMATE OF ESTATE VALUE

1. Net worth (from "Statement of Personal Assets and Liabilities" at end of Chapter 1) $.........
2. Life insurance and other death benefits $.........
3. Minus cash value of life insurance listed on "Statement of Personal Assets and Liabilities" (to avoid double counting)   (.........)
4. Total life insurance and other death benefits (Line 2 minus Line 3)   ....
       Estimated current value of estate (Line 1 plus Line 4) $.........

TRUSTS

Trusts have a variety of advantages. As I've mentioned before, you don't necessarily have to be a billionaire, or even a millionaire, to take advantage of them. Trusts can increase administrative convenience, shelter you from lawsuits and creditors (if it is an irrevocable trust), allow for a speedier inheritance, and, in some cases, reduce your tax burden at the same time. Most importantly, a trust can be tailored to meet almost all of your objectives. For example, a simple will typically gives your assets to your heirs outright. Many people, particularly those who have accumulated or will accumulate a relatively large estate, are uncomfortable with the prospect of their children or spouse receiving all these assets at once with no strings attached. A trust can be set up that will empower the trustee to distribute trust income to beneficiaries according to their needs. This may be particularly useful if you have a disabled child or if you have children of widely differing economic circumstances.

A trust can be created to shift the burden of management to a trusted third party, to transfer property to minors without the need to appoint a guardian, to safeguard your investments against unwise or extravagant spending during your lifetime, or even as a retirement tool to ensure you will have a well-managed fund should you become incapable of managing it yourself. Your attorney may recommend that trusts be used in conjunction with your business as well.

A *revocable living trust* can be a useful estate planning tool even for people of average means. A living trust is usually set up to hold your property, naming yourself as the principal beneficiary. Regardless of your age or mental condition, the trustee is legally bound to act in the beneficiary's best interests according to the trust's instructions. A living trust's immediate advantage is that it can minimize or circumvent probate; if all the assets of the grantor (the person who sets up the trust) are held in the trust, there is nothing to transfer through the will. The trust ensures continuous management of the assets, uninterrupted by death. If the grantor at any point is disabled or otherwise unable to make an important decision concerning the assets, the co-trustee can take responsibility. The granter can appoint a financial adviser as co-trustee if he or she does not wish to manage all the assets while living. A trust provides more assurance than a will that your desires will be carried out; a trust document can specify exact conditions about the distribution of assets (such as at what age a child will receive an inheritance), and can allow the trustee the discretion to withhold or distribute extra assets if prudent or necessary. A living trust is particularly desirable when state probate laws are burdensome.

A person may be unwilling to establish a living trust but may still want to control the way in which the beneficiaries receive the estate after his or her death. This can be accomplished by creating a trust with instructions contained in the will, known as a *testamentary trust.* An example of the use of a testamentary trust was illustrated in this chapter's earlier example entitled "A Simple Will Can Be an Expensive ($235,000) Mistake." If you set up a revocable living trust or a testamentary trust, you can either change or eliminate the trust during your lifetime.

Unlike the revocable trust, an *irrevocable trust* requires you to give up permanently the assets you transfer to it. Since the property in trust is no longer yours, it will be transferred on your death to your heirs without the delays and administrative costs of probate. The best property to put in to an irrevocable trust is that which has appreciation potential—such as stocks and real estate—because if the property increases in value after you transfer it to the trust, the increase will not be subject to estate tax. On the other hand, irrevocable trusts incur legal and administrative fees and, most importantly, you lose control of the assets forever.

Therefore, these trusts are suitable only if you can easily afford to part with the assets.

Other estate planning techniques to be aware of and wary of. Several other techniques can be used as part of the estate planning process. For example, you are probably aware that you can give as much as $10,000 per year to any person without any gift tax implications. Wealthy people do this in order to reduce the size of their taxable estate. Although your children would love you to give them a lot of money each year, you must make sure you have sufficient resources to last you for the rest of your life. How much is sufficient? Most experts suggest that if your estate is less than $1.5 million, you should avoid giving any but nominal gifts to your children and grandchildren. Why so much? A long-term confinement in a nursing home can reduce the size of a retired person's estate dramatically—even to the point of impoverishing the elderly person or couple.

You may think of charitable giving as simply writing out a check to a favorite organization, but there is a variety of ways to donate property to charity in exchange for a lifetime income and a partial income tax deduction. Some people have made good use of these arrangements to provide additional income during retirement, but they must be charitably inclined, because better investment returns can be garnered elsewhere. Two common ways to do this are through either a "charitable gift annuity" or a "pooled income fund." If these interest you, and you have at least $5,000 to $10,000 to donate, check with your favorite charity. They will be more than happy to guide you through the rather complex arrangements.

COMMONLY MADE MISTAKES IN ESTATE PLANNING

Dying without a will or not properly structuring a large estate through the use of trusts are not the only mistakes that can be made in estate planning. This is why it is so essential for you

> Personal financial planning would be a lot easier if we knew when we were going to die.

to use the services of a competent estate planning attorney. The following list describes commonly made estate planning mistakes:

■ While jointly held property may be satisfactory for a relatively small estate, a number of potential disadvantages include a possible double federal estate tax and lack of control over the property once it has passed to the survivor(s). There may be lifetime disadvantages to jointly held property as well, particularly when there is a potential for personal liability arising out of either personal or professional acts.

■ Improperly arranged life insurance can also cause problems in your estate. Life insurance often plays a particularly important role in the estate planning of self-employed professionals and small business owners. If your estate is going to be large enough to incur estate taxes, you should consider the use of an *irrevocable life insurance trust*. At a minimum, you need to ensure that ownership and beneficiary designations on all your life insurance policies are appropriate from the standpoint of your personal wishes as well as estate tax planning.

■ Another problem you may overlook in your estate planning is the need for sufficient liquidity to meet the obligations occasioned by your demise, including probate and administration costs, estate taxes (federal and/or state), and costs of supporting your family and business for a period of time after your death. You need to figure out how much cash and what resources that are readily convertible into cash will be available were you to die today, and compare that with the estimated needs of your family, your business, and your estate.

■ Choosing the wrong executor can also create enormous problems, particularly if the chosen individual is inexperienced or may cause friction among family members. So pay particular attention to choosing an executor who can adequately handle the settlement of your estate or is wise enough to seek professional assistance.

■ If you own property in more than one state, you could create a nightmare for your survivors because this may require probate proceedings in each of the states in which you own property. A properly structured living trust could alleviate this problem. Check with your estate planning attorney.

ADVANCE PLANNING FOR YOUR ADVANCED
YEARS (AND CARING FOR YOUR PARENTS IN THEIRS)

Although we often think of ourselves as a nation of materialists who are unwilling to sacrifice our own comfort to take care of our parents, in fact today an estimated seven to eight million Americans provide personal care to their parents, so the evidence suggests that Americans do care for their elders. But few of us plan ahead effectively and prepare for the probability that our parents will, at least to some extent, rely on us during their old age—and that we, too, will eventually reach an age where we need the assistance of others to carry on our day-to-day activities. In any case, for emotional and financial reasons, anyone with an elderly parent should think about possible action to take if a crisis should happen, so that even if the worst does take place, the consequences will not be needlessly disruptive. Besides, you can plan for your own senior years while you plan your parents'. You're still too young to worry about such matters? That's the point! For now, we'll start with caring for your parents.

Even an elderly parent who appears to be in good health may be having difficulties that require your help. Unpaid bills, unfilled prescriptions, an overdrawn bank account, or other indications of bouts of forgetfulness are all possible first signs that an elderly person's ability to take care of himself or herself may be lessening. If you've noticed any impairments in your elderly parents, encourage them to be checked thoroughly by a doctor. Although you may be inclined to believe the problem is a natural result of aging, it may well be treatable. Many elderly people resist medical evaluation, often out of fear that they may be sent to a nursing home on the basis of the results, so be sure to assure your parents that they will not be forced to make any changes in their lives without their own consent.

While parents are still healthy, it is important that you have a frank discussion with them about plans for and worries about the future. Housing, and the possibility of moving if the present location is inconvenient, is a critical topic. Many retirement homes and other elder care facilities have long waiting lists, so to avoid having an elderly parent placed in an unsatisfactory home because of a sudden illness, you and your parents should discuss alternatives and possibly apply to a home before the need actually arises. Even if your parents are healthy, they should consider any housing decisions in anticipation of possible future health problems.

One of the most important things to plan in advance is how your parents expect to meet any major health care costs. Do they have sufficient health insurance? Remember that Medicare has many gaps in its coverage. It is difficult but prudent to raise the unpleasant issue of what will happen if your parents become incapable of managing their own affairs. They (as well as you) should have durable powers of attorney or similar documents prepared. Ask your parents how well they have been meeting expenses, keeping in mind that they may not wish to reveal any financial problems. Also, be sure your parents have a file, kept in a location known to you, containing copies of their wills, insurance policies, real estate papers, past tax returns, and other important documents.

The elderly parent's future financial situation also needs to be evaluated. Even an elderly parent who is presently financially secure may eventually run into trouble. A retiree's typically fixed income is always in danger of having its purchasing power eroded by inflation; and, of course, medical care and nursing care can reduce anyone's income and savings drastically. It is important to consider what measures you are willing or able to take to assist your parent financially. Even if you are willing to give some of your own money to your parents, you should discuss with them how they are currently managing their own investments. Many elderly people either invest too conservatively or are susceptible to exploitation by unscrupulous individuals.

Many children live a considerable distance away from their parents, which may make assuring that they are well cared for especially difficult. Most cities have agencies available to meet the basic needs of the elderly, from home health care to companionship and escort services. The National Association of Area Agencies on Aging, 600 Maryland Avenue SW, West Wing, Suite 208, Washington, D.C. 20024, lists local agencies. You can write NAAAA to request information on agencies in your parents' locale. Services that can be arranged include:

- Emergency medical response systems
- Daily visits by local residents
- Home care (e.g., laundry, housecleaning, cooking, small repairs, errands, and snow shoveling)
- Legal assistance
- Hot meals (at neighborhood centers or delivered to the home)
- Transportation services
- Day care centers

Further help can be sought through senior citizens centers, religious organizations, welfare services, nursing homes, local branches of the United Way, and major hospital social services departments or elderly outreach programs. If the elderly person requires substantial health-related assistance, a hospital-based social worker is often the best alternative. Of course, in choosing among these plans, parents should be included in all discussions to the extent possible. By all means, make yourself available to assist your elderly parents with any questions or concerns they may have, and remind them regularly of your willingness to help them at any time.

One final comment pertaining to your parents (or you, if you're elderly). The biggest fear that elderly people have today is that they will be wiped out financially if they have to go into a nursing home. This fear often precipitates drastic financial action. You are probably aware of the efforts many elderly take (often at the urging of their children) to rearrange their assets so they can qualify for Medicaid if they have to enter a nursing home. Parents and children should ask themselves if it is worth having the elderly person enter a Medicaid nursing home in order to pass on some assets to children or if it is preferable to use these assets, if necessary, to provide a more satisfactory nursing home environment for the parent.

After reading this chapter, you may still be reluctant to take the action necessary to plan your estate. After all, who wants to contemplate terminal illness, and death—either our own or our parents'? Nevertheless, I can promise that you will feel better after having attended to these important matters, and once you have done so, any future changes in your circumstances or plans will be easy to incorporate in your estate planning documents.

ESTATE ACTION PLAN

CURRENT STATUS

Needs Action	Okay or Not Applicable	
☐	☐	1. Determine your wishes for the ultimate disposition of your estate.
☐	☐	2. Plan carefully for the disposition of your business, coordinate it with other estate planning matters, and incorporate your plans in your estate planning documents.
☐	☐	3. Write an up-to-date will that is consistent with your personal wishes and circumstances.
☐	☐	4. Name an appropriate executor.
☐	☐	5. Prepare and keep up to date a letter of instructions.
☐	☐	6. Establish a durable power of attorney or living trust that protects you in the event of incapacity.
☐	☐	7. Designate guardians for your children and, if applicable, disabled adults.
☐	☐	8. Prepare a living will.
☐	☐	9. Prepare an estimate of your taxable estate.
☐	☐	10. Determine if your estate is sufficiently liquid to meet all needs; if not, take action to increase its liquidity.
☐	☐	11. Make sure that the title in which you hold property is appropriate.

Needs Action	*Okay or Not Applicable*	
☐	☐	12. Any gifts to relatives and/or charitable contributions should be consistent with your financial condition and overall estate planning.
☐	☐	13. If you own property in more than one state, take appropriate actions to minimize probate problems upon your demise.
☐	☐	14. Consider the use of revocable and irrevocable trusts as part of the estate planning process.
☐	☐	15. Inform your family and any other beneficiaries of your plans.
☐	☐	16. Consider the possibility that you will incur substantial uninsured health care costs during retirement.
☐	☐	17. If you have elderly parents, inquire periodically as to the status of their personal finances and estate plans.
☐	☐	18. Be sure that the attorney who handles your estate planning is up to the task. If your estate is quite large or complex, you should retain a highly qualified and experienced estate planning attorney.

Comments: ....
....
....
....

Estate Planning "To Do" List: ....
....
....
....
....
....

9

Achieving Financial Peace of Mind in the 1990s and Beyond: Ten (Relatively) Simple Things to Do

There are so many important matters to attend to in your personal finances that at times it seems overwhelming. You can't do everything, of course, but there are always some things you can do to improve your financial well-being. Good personal financial planning doesn't have to be a time-consuming, daily process. No one in your profession has much spare time anyway. Fortunately, several basic guidelines will help you focus on important financial planning and money management matters. I won't promise you financial nirvana, but if you adhere to the following ten financial planning guidelines, you will be able to enjoy some peace of mind knowing you are well on your way to financial security.

1. *Be happy with what you've got.* People who overextend themselves usually do so in an attempt to maintain a life-style beyond their means. The only way to accumulate wealth is to live *beneath* your means, and the only way to live comfortably beneath your means is to be happy with what you've already got.

2. *Coordinate your personal financial planning with your business planning.* The business and personal financial lives of self-employed professionals and small business owners are inter-

related in several important areas including insurance, investments, taxes, retirement planning, and estate planning. While you certainly need to pay attention to important personal financial planning matters apart from your business, you also must be cognizant of areas where they overlap. For example, you may be able to benefit by obtaining insurance and accumulating retirement funds through your business. On the other hand, business ownership may complicate your estate planning.

3. *Close all gaps in your insurance coverage.* A single gap in your insurance coverage could easily wipe out years of savings and investments and could jeopardize your business. Everyone needs comprehensive and continuous insurance coverage. Independent businesspeople must be especially careful to ensure that they (as well as their businesses) have appropriate insurance coverage since they don't have an employer who would normally provide certain essential insurance coverage.

4. *Don't rely on the sale of your business to provide you with financial security.* Unless you inherit it, marry it, or are one of the lucky few who can sell their business for a large sum, you will never accumulate enough money to achieve retirement security without saving regularly outside of the business. It is inexcusable not to save at least 10 percent of your *gross* (not net) income no matter what your circumstances. If you say you can't do it, you haven't looked hard enough at how you spend your money. If you are lucky enough to withdraw a large sum of money from your business from time to time, save it rather than spend it.

5. *Maintain a balanced investment portfolio that is appropriate to your own financial situation.* Most people invest in extremes, either taking too much risk or too little risk. The best portfolio structure is one that includes stock investments, interest-earning investments, and perhaps real estate investments. Be sure to consider the risk associated with your business in determining what investments are best suited to your circumstances. Your chosen asset allocation should be considered a long-term allocation, one that is not altered materially in response to current market conditions or, worse, the opinions of an "expert."

6. *Develop a reasonable investment strategy and stick with it.* You don't have the time to be an investment expert. Fill your balanced investment portfolio with sensible (some might say dull) investments that you wouldn't mind holding for the rest of your life. Don't overlook the many advantages offered by mutual funds. Above all, be consistent in carrying out your investment strategy.

7. *Take advantage of the tax breaks available to self-employed professionals and small business owners.* By virtue of your ownership of a business, you can take advantage of numerous tax breaks associated with your business activities. On the other hand, don't let income tax saving considerations outweigh more important financial planning matters. Current tax rules require a new and better way of thinking. Rather than asking "Is this going to save me taxes?" you should ask "Is this a worthwhile cost or investment?"

8. *Recognize that it will cost a fortune to retire comfortably, and begin preparing now.* Much of what you do in your year-to-year financial planning is directly or indirectly geared toward assuring you a comfortable retirement. Yet many people still fall short. No matter how young or old you are, don't delay projecting your retirement needs and planning to meet them. Take advantage of the tax-favored retirement plans that are available for independent businesspeople. Be realistic in estimating how much your business will be able to contribute toward your retirement. Most small business owners still have to accumulate considerable personal resources outside of their businesses.

9. *Prepare and keep up-to-date necessary estate planning documents (unless you dislike your heirs).* If you are one of the many who don't yet have a will, a durable power of attorney, and a living will, by all means ask an attorney to prepare them. Believe it or not, you will feel better for having done so. Business owners usually have more complex estate planning needs that require considerable deliberation. Affluent people may benefit from more sophisticated estate planning techniques.

10. *Take control of your personal finances.* Don't rely too much on others (including myself) to tell you what is good for your own situation. You know best. You are undoubtedly preoccupied with your business endeavors, but you still need to devote at least some time to managing your money and your advisers.

Good financial planning begins with good common sense. Financial security may still be a long way off, but as you begin to take control of your financial future, you'll find that many rewards accompany the sacrifices along the way. Don't get discouraged, and always remember that *you* are your own best financial planner. Good luck!

FINANCIAL PLANNING "THINGS TO DO TOMORROW" LIST

Before you put this book away, please write down three things you need to do *now* to help improve your personal finances. The three things don't need to be the most crucial; instead, they should be matters you can accomplish with relative ease, such as arranging with your bank to have some money automatically and regularly withdrawn from your checking account and placed in a savings or investment account. After you have accomplished these three tasks, you'll be encouraged to do more, and you'll be well on your way to a successful financial life.

1. _____
_____
_____

2. _____
_____
_____

3. _____
_____
_____